WOLFGANG C. GÄDEKE was born in Bremen in 1943. He studied Protestant and Catholic theology, and was ordained as a priest of the Christian Community in Stuttgart. He has worked as a priest, a marriage guidance counsellor, taught at the Priests' Seminary in Stuttgart, and held courses on marriage. Since 1990 he has been a director of the Christian Community in North Germany.

Sexuality, Partnership and Marriage

from a spiritual perspective

Wolfgang Gädeke

TEMPLE LODGE

Translated by Heidi Herrmann-Davey (interviews) and William Forward (lectures)

Temple Lodge Publishing
Hillside House, The Square
Forest Row, RH18 5ES

www.templelodge.com

Published by Temple Lodge 1998
Reprinted 2009

Originally published in German by Flensburger Hefte Verlag, Flensburg, Germany. The interview 'Sexuality – The Divided Curtain' appeared in *Flensburger Hefte 20 – Sexualität, Aids, Prostitution*, 1988. The rest of the material is drawn from *Sonderheft 1 – Partnershaft und Ehe*, 1986. Both lectures were held in Söcking, Germany, in October 1985

A catalogue record for this book is available from the British Library

ISBN 978 0 904693 99 7

Cover by Andrew Morgan, incorporating 'Satan watching the endearments of Adam and Eve' by William Blake (Museum of Fine Arts, Boston)

Typeset by DP Photosetting, Aylesbury, Bucks.
Printed and bound in Great Britain

Contents

PART TWO: LECTURES

Publisher's Foreword

Some people claim that men and women are fundamentally different. But what are the differences? Is female sexuality really that different from the male or are they, in fact, essentially the same? — as is also often suggested today. What is sexuality? Are children sexual beings? Is there a paradoxical element in human sexuality that is likely to destroy the love between two people?

With such questions as the above, Wolfgang Weirauch, a co-founder and editor of *Flensburger Hefte* — a German periodical which seeks to cast light on modern questions through spiritual insight — interviewed the priest and marriage counsellor Wolfgang Gädeke. The results, which were published in two issues of *Flensburger Hefte* together with lectures by Gädeke and other supplementary material, have received a phenomenal amount of attention. The public demand has been such that the special issue of the journal on partnership and marriage, for example, has already gone into its fifth edition, and continues to sell!

We are pleased to make these valuable interviews and lectures from Wolfgang Gädeke available to the English reader. Together, they constitute perhaps the most strikingly successful attempt to deal with questions of sexuality, partnership and marriage from a modern, spiritual perspective.

We have arranged the material in the book to make it as accessible as possible (not necessarily in chronological order) and to aid a smooth reading of the text. Thus, the interviews have been gathered together in Part One, and the lectures in Part Two. Those readers who wish to begin with a scientific overview of Gädeke's thoughts on sexuality may wish to start with the first lecture in Part Two. (The areas of repetition between this lecture and the second interview have not been edited in the interests of maintaining the organic wholeness of both pieces.)

For those readers not conversant with the inspiration behind Gädeke's words, it should be stated that he is a student of the work of the Austrian-born philosopher, educationalist and seer Rudolf Steiner (1861–1925), whose ground-breaking 'science of the spirit', Anthroposophy, has regrettably been largely ignored by mainstream twentieth-century thought. Steiner set about publishing and speaking of the results of his clairvoyant investigations, so-called 'spiritual research', in many books and thousands of lectures, many of which have now been published in English translation. He also founded the Anthroposophical Society.

The Christian Community, of which Gädeke is a priest, was set up at the instigation of Friedrich Rittelmeyer — an eminent Lutheran preacher from Berlin — as an attempt to breathe fresh life into religion based on a celebration of renewed Christian sacraments. (Rudolf Steiner aided and encouraged Rittelmeyer in this initiative, but did not see it as his personal task to found a religious movement.)

SG, London, February 1998

PART ONE
INTERVIEWS

1. Sexuality – The Divided Curtain

Wolfgang Weirauch: *The emergence of AIDS has led to a far more open discussion of sexuality; in Germany the well-known feminist author Alice Schwarzer has initiated a new debate on pornography. In this interview with you I would like to establish some of the fundamental aspects of what might be referred to as sexuality and gender.*

Let us start with the difference between a human being and a plant. How is a being such as the plant, which is devoid of any desire, differentiated from the soul-imbued human being?

Wolfgang Gädeke: Compared with the mineral the plant has certain characteristics which we refer to as growth and reproduction. This is not an additive-quantitative kind of growth but a qualitative one; unlike a stone, which can only manifest in its given structure and form, the plant grows qualitatively from within. This growth is associated with metabolic processes and many other factors which result in different leaf forms, and finally, in a blossom which is of a new and completely different nature. The plant does not possess what we might call sensations or inherent movement – in contrast to animal and man. For sensations, inherent movement, feelings and emotions as well as drives and desires are the preserve of the soul-imbued creature – animal and man.

Sympathy and antipathy

W.W.: *Let's have a look at two human soul gestures: sympathy and antipathy. Could you describe the essential qualities of the gesture of sympathy?*

W.Gädeke: Sympathy is the gesture by which the inner

space or inner world of soul-imbued beings opens up to the outside, to other souls or impressions; sympathy is a gesture of opening the soul.

W.W.: How would you define the opposite gesture, i.e. antipathy?

W.Gädeke: Antipathy is the gesture in which the soul closes itself off, thereby separating other soul beings from one's own. However, antipathy is not something negative although it is frequently used in a negative sense. It is a necessary gesture of the soul, for if we continually confronted the world in sympathy, in a gesture of opening-up, we would never find ourselves. We would not feel ourselves either, and we would not be capable of making judgements or attaining a state of soul autonomy.

W.W.: Both forces are one-sided polarities then?

W. Gädeke: Both are one-sided forces; for example, it can be observed in small children, when they go through their first phase of defiance, that the act of refusing or denying in relation to another person serves the strengthening of the experience of self. This shows that the force of antipathy can be very beneficial and useful. Therefore it would be wrong to view sympathy as positive and antipathy as negative.

W.W.: What are the primary connections between these polarities and other forces of the human soul?

W. Gädeke: First of all it could be said that sympathy and antipathy are fundamental feelings, basic dynamics of the soul. As antipathy is mainly present whenever we feel ourselves as autonomous beings vis-à-vis the world, it primarily occurs when we perceive this outer world, when we observe it and form ideas about it, think about it and form judgements. We need the forces of antipathy in order to take this kind of stance towards the world. They work in all our thoughts, concepts and perceptions.

W.W.: And which are the powers of soul that the forces of sympathy connect with?

W. Gädeke: Sympathy is the force which connects us with other beings and as such it naturally acts particularly strongly when we perform any such act of opening up, for example when we greet another person with a handshake, or affect the world through our work. All this is brought about by the activity of our metabolic/limb system on which our will is based. Sympathy works in the will because every will action, every deed is a connection with the world. Whether I eat, dig over my garden or write a letter – I impress something on the world and in doing so I move away from myself and turn to the world. This is the fundamental gesture of sympathy in willing and doing.

W.W.: *Do these two soul gestures affect the etheric and physical body of man?*

W. Gädeke: Of course these two constituents of the human being are characterized by inherent forces working in them: the life forces as well as the laws of the mineral world. If we look at the life forces of breathing in and breathing out we can see that these are related to sympathy and antipathy. When we breathe in we take something of the world into ourselves and lock it up within us; this is a gesture related to antipathy. I don't want to say that breathing in represents antipathy, but in the realm of the life processes it is a related process. When I breathe out I communicate to the world something that was previously within me – a gesture related to sympathy. In addition, breathing and nutrition are processes of the physical body and in this way the processes I described work there also.

W.W.: *Now there are different types of person, aren't there: those predominantly guided by antipathy and others who tend to be almost totally absorbed by forces of sympathy?*

W.Gädeke: In the case of people who have not developed the power of their ego and are constantly torn between sympathy and antipathy, two different types manifest. Those who predominantly live with the forces of sympathy, who are totally related to their environment, who only feel good when they are in company with others, who cannot bear being alone; for example the kind of people psychologists call over-protective mothers, who only feel that they exist when they can help others at all times, who want to be always there for others and 'never expect anything for themselves'. There is no 'I'-quality in this kind of life orientation.

A very tragic form of the opposite may be seen in autistic children who are completely locked up within their own soul nature; in this case there is a sort of imprisonment due to the over-dominance of antipathy forces. Of course adults can also manifest in this way: people who find it extremely difficult to make contact, who cannot connect themselves properly with anything in the world, who remain self-related and introverted. In such cases there is also a predominance of antipathy forces.

Of course these are soul types and not personality types for it is an essential feature of the 'I' that it guides these two forces. That's why the 'I' is referred to in the New Testament as the key of David which has the power to unlock and no one may lock, and which locks and no one may unlock. This basically describes the fact that an autonomous authority handles the functions of unlocking and locking, and that it does so in accordance with its own inherent laws and not as a result of predominating forces of sympathy or antipathy.

Now we have arrived at an important characterization of the function of the 'I' in general: that of opening the soul or closing it, of judging what is taken into the soul and what is not, and what is let out of the soul and what is not. When I decide on what I will speak about and what I will keep to myself I avail myself of a function of my 'I' and not of a soul function.

Sexuality of the young child?

W.W.: *Let us consider the human being in the first seven years; what is the configuration of our constituent members[1] in that period?*

W. Gädeke: At birth the child is only born in the physical sense. In relation to its other constituent members it is not yet born, i.e. not yet independent, as Rudolf Steiner describes in his *Education of the Child*. Initially the child is obviously dependent on being nourished by the mother's body, albeit no longer from within through the blood, but from outside through the mother's milk, and is still in an immediate connection with the mother. This is expressed in the fact that the child's life-forces are still largely unborn and dependent on the life forces of the mother. With regard to the soul, too, it may be observed in small children that the range of expressions is very limited. The infant already displays inherent movement, a first ability to perceive and feel, but most of the other soul functions don't develop until later.

Joy, smiling or deeply-felt sympathy, these things are not present from the start. Also the 'I'-functions don't evolve until later, for example eye-coordination, coordination of the hand movements for taking hold of things, and of the leg movements for walking etc. Basically all these are functions controlled by the 'I'. The soul as well as the spiritual nature of a small child are still very strongly connected with the parents and the child's environment. It is only during the 'difficult' or 'defiant' stage – around the third year – that the child gradually begins to detach itself from its environment and starts to experience itself as somewhat separate, with feelings of its own.

W.W.: Sigmund Freud refers to an infantile sexuality encompassing an oral and an anal phase. Why is it not appropriate, in terms of the anthroposophical picture of man, to speak of sexuality in relation to this phase of life?

W. Gädeke: This depends on how sexuality is defined. Of course a small child will go through a phase of sticking everything into its mouth, that's perfectly obvious, but the question is whether such behaviour should be described as sexual. Furthermore, it goes without saying that a child will explore all the parts of his body — also the sexual organs — and will do this all in a playful manner. However, no one would refer to a 'heel phase' just because the child concentrates his playful discovery on his heels for a certain time. I would say that there is absolutely no difference in the child's attention for the various parts of the body, initially they are all of equal interest. Hence it is premature to refer to sexuality in this context.

W.W.: If children in their first seven years are actively encouraged to play with their genitals, to live out that so-called infantile sexuality, or if children are actually abused by adults — how does this affect them later on, say between twenty-one and twenty-eight?

W. Gädeke: The mere fact that children would actually have to be encouraged to relate to their genitals in a sexual way — it is generally not something they would do of their own accord — indicates that this is likely to result in deeply problematic situations. The child is forced to perceive his own body and this will result in a loss of interest in the world. A child wants to grow into the world, find out about the world, and any kind of enhanced self-perception will prevent this. Therefore it ought to be the main focus of the up-bringing of a child to encourage the child to explore the world with his hands — in the literal sense — and not himself.

When real sexual acts, in the adult sense, are performed with a child — such as abuse by a relative — and it does not have to be rape — then this is one of the most atrocious things that can be done to a child. In my marriage-counselling group I have met a lady who has dealt with this kind of problem a lot, and I also know the accounts of people who have experienced sexual abuse as children; such abuse has terrible effects in the fourth seven-year-span! It affects their marriage in many different ways, it is a real misfortune, for it is very difficult to heal the wounds suffered in this way. As far as I can tell the soul damage in such cases is practically irreparable.

W.W.: *Could you say more about this?*

W.Gädeke: I had a couple, for example, and they were very well-disposed to one another. They were both exploring the idea of marriage from many aspects, but the young woman had been abused by her father for many years; hence she had a strong revulsion for any kind of physical touch, but she also longed for love, tenderness and a feeling of security. To witness this contradiction in her soul nearly tore my heart apart. The young man had tried really hard to accommodate her, he was very patient; I have to admit that I was unable, as he had been, to help the situation through counselling.

W.W.: *We got a similar message from another of our interviewees who spoke about the early childhood experiences of most prostitutes. Most of them had their first sexual experience with adults, and in connection with money.*

W.Gädeke: That's very interesting! I consider it totally wrong to associate these early childhood experiences with the child's 'own sexuality', as Sigmund Freud and others do; at least as far as the first seven-year-span is concerned.

W.W.: *How does a child relate to its body in these early years? Does it relate to its genitals differently than to the rest of its body?*

W. Gädeke: I don't think so. I certainly have not observed anything like that with my own children.

W.W.: *Does something like a sense of shame occur?*

W. Gädeke: That is different with every child.

The incisive change in the ninth year

W.W.: *Could you briefly describe how the human being's constituent members are configured in the second seven-year-phase, in contrast to the first? What are the changes?*

W. Gädeke: The change of teeth, at approximately the seventh year, marks the beginning of what Rudolf Steiner describes as the second birth. This refers to the birth of the etheric body; it means that the child—in terms of its life forces—becomes independent of parents and environment. As far as the opposite sex is concerned, things remain relatively normal for a while. The children will, of course, discover the different nature of the other sex's physical body, and they will go about it with a certain amount of curiosity, but if one manages to handle this in a matter-of-fact manner, without making a taboo of it or blocking it off by moral precepts of some kind, one will find that it is nothing but an interest in the other human being. At the threshold from the first to the second seven-year-cycle one will often find children engaging in the famous 'doctor and nurses' kind of play; it is an interest in the other human being but not, at this stage, the type of interest that awakens in the third seven-year-cycle, which is directed at the sexual nature of the other.

W.W.: In other words, it's not appropriate to speak of sexuality in relation to the second seven-year-period?

W. Gädeke: No, it's not really. None of the bodily functions associated with adult sexuality manifest at that stage, such as all the glandular functions—the germ glands are not yet productive—and these are important foundations of sexuality.

W.W.: I have been told of various sexual experiences around the ninth year, of masturbation as well as of experiences with the opposite sex, and these were said to have been arousing. What do you make of that?

W. Gädeke: It is interesting that you mention the ninth year, because it can be observed that this is the time when children start to separate themselves off from the other sex. Until the ninth year children will—unless something different is imposed from outside—be perfectly at ease alongside the other sex. For example, they will equally invite girls and boys to their birthday parties without any question whatsoever, for the sole reason that they like them.

But this often changes after the ninth year, something quite incisive happens, and the children begin to sense strongly the different natures of the two genders. At school you can observe that the boys will refer to the girls as 'silly girls' and the girls start speaking about 'stupid boys'. At that age something of a separation takes place; but even if things like masturbation occur, it is solely a nerve process, not a glandular process.

W.W.: Can this nerve process trigger a sense of arousal?

W. Gädeke: Yes, it can. That is possible! But it does not come from within, it has to be triggered from outside first.

The third seven-year-period: a constant experience of slight pain

W.W.: Let's talk about the third seven-year-cycle; what changes after puberty in the behaviour of girls and boys towards one another?

W. Gädeke: The separation which arises during the ninth year is now gradually reversed. This means that a kind of attraction of the sexes once more emerges, the opposite sex becomes interesting again. What is far more important, however, is that the third birth, as Rudolf Steiner called it, comes to pass now; in other words that the soul forces become independent and a strong inward orientation begins. Many children start to keep a diary; most young people, independent of their social background, will experience intense loneliness, with sadness and melancholia pervading the soul, but on the other hand also feelings of being in love and so forth. The bodily changes are accompanied by a deep transformation of the soul nature, and the reproductive organism fully matures.

W.W.: To elucidate the fact that sexual or earthly maturity is part of a comprehensive process I would like to present the following explanations of Rudolf Steiner:

However, as a result of the fact that man is not sufficiently interested in the world around him he is thrown
back upon himself; and then he starts to hatch all sorts
of things inside. And it must be said in general: if you
look at the fundamental ills of our civilization today,
you find that they essentially consist of people being
exceedingly engaged with their own selves, in that they
generally do not spend a major part of their free time in
dealing with the world but rather concern themselves
with how they are feeling, and what is ailing them. Of
course it is permissible, when it is called for, to occupy
oneself with such concerns; when you are ill it is even
essential to do so. But people are not just occupied with
themselves when they are ill but also when they are
more or less well. And the least favourable age for this
kind of self-preoccupation is the age between the 14th,
15th and the 21st year. During that age the ability to
discern, which comes to flower in that period, should be
directed to the way the world works in all areas of life.
The world must increasingly become so interesting to
the young person that it does not even occur to him to
turn away his attention from the world to the extent of
becoming occupied solely with his own nature. For we
all know that in our subjective experience pain becomes
more intense if we continually dwell on it—not the hurt
caused in an objective sense, but the pain felt becomes
the more intense the more we think about it. In a certain
sense, the very best medicine for overcoming a particular pain is persuading oneself not to think about it. It
should be considered that what develops in the young
person precisely between the 15th, 16th and the 20th,
21st year is not unlike the sensation of pain. The process
of working one's way into the powers of the astral body
which is becoming free in the physical body, is in actual
fact a continuous experience of slight pain. What one
senses there will immediately encourage one to become

concerned with one's own self if one is not sufficiently distracted by interest in the world outside.[2]

W. Gädeke: It's perfectly understandable that a human being in full possession of his soul forces – and this applies at the 14th year when the soul has been born – will concern himself with this powerful inner world in many different ways. For the soul *is* the inner world! Feelings, emotions, drives, desires ... they all entail a preoccupation with self! The processes of being preoccupied with one's own self are indeed natural, but not very productive. That's why Rudolf Steiner encouraged a pedagogy where the soul processes of young people during this particular age are directed outward as strongly as possible in order to encourage an interest in the world, a capacity for discernment and so forth. In this way the soul can be re-connected with the world. If this does not happen the antipathy forces will dominate because the person concerned shuts himself off. This is one of the dangers inherent in the third seven-year-period: the young person becomes so hermit-like that his only concern is his own self; this can end up in an excessive concern with just one's own body.

W.W.: That means that the human being is generally more strongly inclined to antipathy during the third seven-year-period, and that the forces of sympathy, the interest for the world, need to be encouraged?

W. Gädeke: That's a way of putting it, yes indeed.

W.W.: Could you name some of the main problems of a modern youth between 14 and 21 years of age who is exclusively pre-occupied with himself instead of engaging with the world?

W. Gädeke: One striking example would be the 16-year-old boy walking or even cycling around with a dreamy expression and a Walkman round his head. You can clearly see in his eyes that he is not open to the world at all. Such a Walkman may be a nice accessory but when it becomes an essential part of one's constitution it strongly contributes to the risk inherent in that age: becoming totally preoccupied with oneself. The young person experiences nothing but his own soul and body states through this exposure to sound. For in reality it is not a case of enjoying the music but rather the effect of the music on oneself. It is similar with chewing gum and smoking: the essential feature is the perception of self. It is not by chance that smoking is often taken up during this phase of life. This has nothing to do with moralizing—it's simply a fundamental gesture of the third seven-year-period: everything that leads to a perception and an experience of one's own self is natural in this phase of life, but at the same time problematic in that it ultimately separates the person from his fellows and the world at large.

Instinct—drive—desire

W.W.: In the third seven-year-period the desire nature is liberated; is it possible to separate desire from drive and instinct?

W. Gädeke: It is a differentiation Rudolf Steiner has made in the context of Waldorf education. He showed that the animal's will—frequently very wisely—acts as instinct, e.g. as migrating instinct in birds or as a drive to build a nest or a cave and so forth. With many animals this is a very sophisticated and highly developed activity. There is a will involved which works inexorably through the animal's organism, its body, and which cannot be activated or used consciously. A garden spider can only spin its web as it is accustomed: it will never, out of its own initiative, suddenly make it square or rectangular. It is an absolutely unfree will which is tied to a purpose, and yet capable of supreme accomplishments. Rudolf Steiner calls this will which is tied to the physical organism, instinct.

'Drive' on the other hand, denotes the will manifesting in the realm of the life forces. This may be observed in the plant world. Something grows inside and manifests out-wardly as growth, encompassing spatial enlargement and expansion. Neither drive nor instinct are necessarily accompanied by desire, as is clearly expressed in the plant, for it would be utter nonsense to assert that the plant experiences pleasure at the sprouting of a bud.

However, the situation is different in man and animal. Both have desire, i.e. both seek for certain pleasurable experiences of the soul which are related to what we have termed 'drive'. This brings us to a first difference between men and women; for in the man something grows inside as in the plant, and it steadily accumulates and drives to the outside, it must get out, like a sprouting bud; I'm thinking of the incessant formation of new sperm cells. This is primarily a driving process. It becomes desire when we actively wish to provoke this process because we want to experience the process of pleasure associated with it. But the process as such is a drive.

In the case of the woman and her sexual make-up there is no biological foundation for such a self-perpetuating drive. For the single ovum that matures over a month doesn't represent a significant growth process, and it would be difficult to attribute a process of 'driving' to the ovum's eventual slide from the ovary. Of course, some-thing is driven out later on but this is not of a pleasurable nature, on the contrary. Nor is desire connected with the process.

The difference between female and male sexuality

W.W.: In a recent reader's letter to a leading German news magazine a sexual scientist contributed as follows to the current pornography debate: 'Until there is a real understanding of the multifaceted nature of sexuality, and of the fact that there is no significant difference between male and female sexuality [...] there will doubtless be no end to the absurd attempts to see unwanted political force and the actual suppression of women in terms of an over-simplified pornography debate, in which not even the concepts of power and force (in either their positive or negative sense) have been properly defined.' What do you think of the view that there is no difference between female and male sexuality?

W. Gädeke: In view of everything I have learned as a marriage counsellor I consider this assumption to be no more than an ideology which postulates that there must be no difference between female and male sexuality. Experience speaks against this. The biological basis, the drive, is fundamentally different in man and woman. If we define sexuality as sexual union or sexual activity it is a process which involves glands and nerves, for women and men alike. From the point-of-view of the drive's origin, however, the glandular process clearly dominates in the man, but also the nerve activation is far stronger in the case of the man. This is even expressed in the form of the organs; it can be seen in the comparison of the testicle with the clitoris that the nerve centres are far larger in the former; and in the case of sportswomen who are administered lots of hormones an enlargement of the clitoris ensues, with a resultant stronger sex drive. In other words, the nerve processes are far greater in the case of the man as a result of what is inherent in the organism itself; and this equally applies to the glandular activity. So the fact that sexuality is different in woman and man is already conditioned by the organs.

W.W.: *But sexuality cannot be reduced to the workings of the organs, desire plays an essential part, doesn't it? How about the difference between woman and man in this realm?*

W. Gädeke: The realm of desire is related to the soul, but here, too, men and women are different. This manifests in the different approaches one may observe when a relationship first develops between a man and a woman: in general, the man will be the first to urge it along towards sex; the man's desire is far more strongly orientated to the physical, and he experiences the biological foundation of his drive far more intensely than the woman. The woman does not experience the maturing of the ovum and its descent from the ovary in the same way in which a man experiences his own drive through his sexual organs. Therefore, the man's experience impinges more directly on his consciousness. That does not mean that a woman has no desire, but it is of a different nature. Insofar as it is directed at the body at all it is rather orientated to the expression of the eyes and the face, the voice, the hands and above all the mood of soul connected with the body. To sum up, one could perhaps say that the woman desires the man's soul whereas the man primarily desires the woman's body and that his desire attaches much more strongly to the woman's sexual features.

W.W.: There are two points in our discussions about marriage and partnership [see following chapters] which have aroused a lot of criticism. Strangely enough these critical comments came mainly from women although women fared a lot better in these considerations. Firstly, there is criticism of the over-emphasis of the mother's role. And secondly – and this concerns us now – we have been told that the very assertions you were making just now are not accepted by a lot of women. These women don't consider it possible that their desire should only be directed to the man's soul and not to his body; it is pointed out that women's desire for sexual activity equals that which is generally assumed for men.

W. Gädeke: My remarks should not be taken to imply that women have no sexual desire, for example a desire to reach an orgasm; of course this desire exists but it cannot be compared to the man's desire.

W.W.: How do you know that?

W. Gädeke: I know it from the numerous conversations I conduct in the context of marital counselling with various couples; they invariably show that it is a very common problem that men wish to satisfy their drive far more often than women. It is conceivable that only a peculiar type of woman seeks me out as marriage counsellor, but so far my assumption about the differences of male and female sexuality have not yet been refuted by anyone and in addition it is borne out by other literature as well as biological conditions. At present I do not see any reason to believe that it is not so. But it should not be expressed in absolute terms, in the sense of disseminating the view that women are totally free of physical desire. Furthermore a woman's desire—now you'll stone me or declare me an old fuddy-duddy—always involves an urge to have a child, half-consciously or completely unconsciously; a woman has a physical drive towards motherhood. A man has at best a wish to become a father, but there is no respective physical drive. That is a big difference; a wish resides entirely in the soul, but a drive is something physical. The man has a drive to get rid of his sperm but he does not have a drive to become a father.

Men and women love differently

W.W.: *There is an indication by Rudolf Steiner which is very pertinent to this:*

A woman's love is very different from that of a man. In a woman love really originates in the imagination and it is always engaged in forming pictures. A woman never loves a man just as he is, standing there before her in ordinary humdrum life—please forgive me for spelling it out but, after all, men are not exactly of the kind a healthy imagination could fall in love with—in a woman's love there is always something more, she weaves into her love the ideal she has received as heaven's gift. A man, on the other hand, loves in a wishful way; a man's love is always tinged with desire. This differentiation has to be made, no matter whether it shows itself more in an idealistic or a realistic sense. The highest ideal can still encompass ideal desires; and what is most instinctive and sense-related can be a product of the imagination. But this is the radical difference between a man's love and a woman's love. A woman's love is steeped in imagination; a man's love is steeped in desire. In that they are able to form something which harmonizes in life.[3]

W. Gädeke: This is a fundamental statement of Rudolf Steiner about the different ways men and women love. Of course there is an imaginative element in the love of a young man who, in the first flurry of being in love, worships his beloved like a princess, and there can be aspects of desire in a young girl's being-in-love, but generally it can be said that a man's love is characterized by wish or desire. He wants to take possession of what is there, in the present, namely the beautiful girl. Whereas the girl always lives with the imaginary picture of what she thinks the male is to become one day. This really is something which many women today experience with a great deal of suffering: the fact that the man as he appears today is by no means that loveable. This is the reason why women have something of a basic 'pedagogical eros' vis-à-vis men. They are never content with how the men are at present. Many women want to speed the man's development along; on the most primitive level this is the woman who incites her man to further his career. Of course it also manifests at far higher levels, for example in the case of an artist who owes his own development to the encouraging, transforming and inspiring nature of his woman partner. It should not be regarded one-sidedly.

But the quotation of Rudolf Steiner you have just read out is tremendously illuminating about the characteristic differences between male and female love. After all, when problems arise in a relationship it is often the case that the woman reproaches the man with still being as he always has been, with not having changed at all; whereas most men will complain to their wives that they have completely changed, that they were very different in the past when they married them. Most men want to have back the little submissive beautiful girl of the olden days; women want men to get their act together, finally, and grow up.

The paradoxical nature of sexuality

W.W.: How would you define the concept of sexuality?
W.Gädeke: I would like to reserve the term sexuality for the actual sexual act or activity, without the wider interpretation it has in Freudian psychoanalysis in which many other things are referred to by this term which have nothing directly to do with it. I would like sexuality to be understood as referring to that which happens between people by the agency of their sexual organs.
W.W.: You referred earlier to the inherently paradoxical nature of sexuality; what do you mean by that?
W.Gädeke: I cannot actually base what I am going to say on a direct indication of Rudolf Steiner, but I imagine it will be understood. One needs to differentiate between what happens in the soul and in the body during sexual activity. The sexual union in itself is a gesture of sympathy. Sympathy in as far as one strives away from oneself towards the other, opening up not only in soul but also in body, for example by spreading one's arms. It's difficult to unite sexually with one's arms or legs crossed. This physical gesture of opening up applies in principle to man and woman alike: one opens up, turns towards the other, merges right into the other. These gestures of sympathy and openness are gestures of warmth and attention, right until the actual climax of the flowing over of the seminal fluid, which is also a gesture of sympathy and devotion.
W.W.: Do you relate this to man and woman alike?

W. Gädeke: Yes I do, because the basic gesture is the same for both, for you will find partial aspects of this gesture in the entire sexual act. So it can be said that the physical sexual union of man and woman is very much an expression of soul sympathy, of attention and affection, even love.

On the other hand the soul's part in this is that we desire something, want to have something. The problem is that during the physical act we hardly perceive and experience the other person in our soul because we are almost exclusively tied up with perceiving our own physical state. When we look at another person and speak with him or her, we also encounter that person physically, but the physical aspect recedes into the background and is usually only a mediator, a bridge from soul to soul. However, at the very moment when we touch one another physically, especially in the case of having sex, we no longer experience the other, we don't experience the sexual touch as a bridge to the other but rather experience our own physical state; and we enjoy that. But this enjoyment is a desire.

In the third chapter of his *Theosophy* Rudolf Steiner speaks about desire; it is connected with the soul, and is composed of sympathy and antipathy, with the latter forces predominating. The forces of antipathy bring it about that we only experience ourselves. Insofar as desire goes along with sexuality – and considering the way the human being is configured today, it invariably does – the sexual act separates us in soul from the other human being. I do not mean sexuality in terms of the physical process but in terms of its soul-desire aspect. It is the desire aspect with its inherent forces of antipathy which separates us from the other, whereas the physical part of it with its sympathy gesture unites us with the other. That is the inherent paradox of sex!

W.W.: What conclusions do you draw from this contradiction?

W.Gädeke: In the first place this is just a description of the facts. The consequence of these facts is that pure sex will gradually lead to greater and greater separation when nothing else is done to establish a connection in soul.

W.W.: That's pretty evident!

W.Gädeke: What do you mean by evident? Clearly immense numbers of people have experienced this, but have they understood it? The concepts outlined above enable one to understand why it is inevitably so.

Chronos devours his children

W.W.: So far I have understood you to say that people who no longer have a soul relationship will become increasingly cut-off from one another if all they practise is sex. In other words, if there is nothing else, sex won't bring anything about. But how is it with sexuality for people who love each other and have a soul relationship; will sex nevertheless introduce an alienating element into their soul union?

W.Gädeke: This separation or alienation does not only happen when people don't love each other any more, it also occurs when their love still exists. Unless they cultivate real soul connections in other areas apart from their sex life the forces of antipathy inherent in sexual desire will kill off the last shreds of sympathy in the soul's disposition. Chronos eats up his children; this is a mythological picture of the process. Love, insofar as it becomes sexuality, devours itself.

W.W.: If I understand you aright your comments are by no means confined to relationships that no longer work; you are saying that sexuality works its way like a kind of built-in destructive element, a 'time-bomb', even into good love relationships?

W.Gädeke: Quite so! It is plain that this 'time-bomb' ticks away relentlessly and inevitably. When the two partners concerned don't cultivate community on a soul and spiritual level, it will separate them. But if the people concerned nourish their relationship in soul and spirit, the decisive factor will be whether the community arising out of that is strong enough to balance the antipathy forces inherent in each one's desire, time after time.

W.W.: Do you consider the forces of antipathy inherent in desire so strong that they can work in such a destructive and alienating manner? After all, it is also quite possible to become more close with another human being during a sexual act!

W.Gädeke: In my view this is calculated optimism or else an advertising hoax.

W.W.: Neither – Nor!

W.Gädeke: I venture to call into question that one may really become close through sex alone.

W.W.: Another of the criticisms of our interviews about marriage and partnership – incidentally from women – has been that in real life, so they say, far less importance is attached to what we called 'a hot drink together in the evening' (what is meant is a brief shared period between the partners every day when they tell each other about the day's happenings and thereby share in the other's soul content – see page 118) than to sex, when it comes to establishing closeness between two partners.

W.Gädeke: Yes, that's right, it may well be experienced in this way during the first two years of a relationship, because that's roughly how long the natural forces of 'being-in-love' last, but then they are usually used up unless something new in the realm of the soul and spiritual is built up. I am not asserting that the sex act is devoid of forces which lead to closeness; on the contrary, these deeper forces are indeed the physical and life forces. Of course, sexuality also encompasses an experience of union, of closeness, but experience teaches us that this is rapidly eaten up by the other component, i.e. the forces of antipathy; after two years it's all over.

W.W.: Could you define this a bit more? I am still finding it difficult to grasp in which way the antipathy forces work destructively in sexual desire, and in which specific ways – anthroposophically speaking – they attack the various members of the person and the partner concerned.

W. Gädeke: The more one is wrapped up with oneself the less open one can be towards the partner. Sex, however, is a predominantly self-related concern even though it involves another person. The process of sex carries an inherent and continual risk of degrading the other to an object, namely an object of one's own satisfaction. That's why sexuality occurs in so many different guises in which this becomes very apparent and where the other clearly is nothing but an object. But that is sexuality, too. Indeed, the fact that this is possible, and the range of possibilities and extreme nature of some of these phenomena—think of promiscuous individuals who change partners daily—shows that the sex relationship can take on forms which no longer suggest a comprehensive human relationship but where the other is nothing more than a momentary object. Such examples make it undeniably clear. What may be observed in prostitution, in pornography and so forth—and the feminist movement has again pointed to this emphatically—is that women are degraded to mere objects. All this is inherent in sexuality in seed form. If it was not so it could not manifest in such crass forms. It is this element of sexuality, this way of making objects of one another, which separates people.

W.W.: This all makes sense but it sounds very absolute. One might equally argue that every act of thinking invariably involves an act of dying – but the latter is right and good and necessary for the act of thinking. The process of dying is part of the process of thinking. But your statements about sexuality seem to imply that it would be better to stop all sexual activity altogether.

W.Gädeke: This is not what I intended to imply. I just wish to draw attention to the fact that sexuality is inherently paradoxical. And I wish to emphasize that no amount of utilitarian optimism can do away with this fact. Anyone can say, for example, that it's necessary for everyone to live in accordance with their nature, etc., but you will find that it doesn't work. Anyone who chooses to live merely in accordance with the nature of sexuality will find that he or she will become very estranged, as a human being, from the other. For sexuality – and this is the problem of the topic we are discussing now – is only a small constituent of the overall human; and if it is made the central issue, people's problems become even more severe. As a matter of fact we are speaking about sexuality in its pure form, without considering any meeting in soul or spirit between people. On this premise it is appropriate to speak as I have done.

W.W: Let's consider an actual case: Two people have been living together for a number of years, the initial state of being in love has passed, they have sexual intercourse at an average rate ...

W.Gädeke: ... twice a week according to Luther.

W.W.: ... would you confirm that the forces of antipathy within these people's sexual desires are not so powerful as to potentially destroy the relationship which both partners also nurture on a level of soul and spirit!?

W.Gädeke: So far I have only addressed that part of a relationship which is there naturally. Your question brings us to the idea of cultivating a relationship; in other words *culture* as opposed to *nature.*

W.W.: Could we first look at another aspect: we agree that sexuality is not the be-all and end-all of a relationship; hence the forces of antipathy inherent in sexual desire by no means represent the totality of antipathy forces at play in two partners' everyday life together but only part of the total. It is, after all, a basic characteristic of the human being today to be self-orientated, to lie to himself and to exploit the other in an egotistic manner – all this is a part of everyday life with others. Why do you give such prominence to the antipathy forces of sexual desire which only represent a partial aspect of the human being's entire antipathy forces?

W.Gädeke: Of course all that you mention also has a decisive and troublesome role in human life, but sexuality is a process which reaches very deeply indeed, for the simple reason that there is no other occasion when we are physically *that* close – even from a purely outer point of view. That's why the forces referred to have a much more immediate effect. Furthermore — mind you, this is an almost impermissible thought today — the process is connected with the great world processes of procreation. Today people are more and more intent on denying everything that is connected with procreation. The mere fact that it is becoming increasingly necessary to concentrate on preventing a procreation demonstrates how strongly sexuality is, by nature, connected with procreation. These are forces which reach far beyond our consciousness and our abilities. In this realm we are confronted with powers — not only in the soul realm but also in the physical processes — which do not lend themselves to comparison with others.

Reaching for the soul of the other through physical contact!

W.W.: *Let us now deal with the cultural aspect: How does one handle sexuality in a relationship in such a way that the forces of sexuality don't predominate?*
W.Gädeke: Amongst other things it is essential to counterbalance the concentration on the sexual aspect, which occurs very quickly, by making an effort to deal with one another in a more all-encompassing manner — not only in the areas of the soul and spiritual but also in the physical sphere. I am thinking of what is generally referred to as kissing and cuddling today. It's something which has been affirmed without question by all the women with whom I have spoken in the context of marital counselling: kissing and cuddling is more important to them than sex. That means that their physical desire is more inclined towards a wholesome physical encounter as opposed to a purely sexual one; one might call this eroticism. The essential feature of kissing and cuddling is that one is not so intensely captivated by one's own physical perception but remains

more open towards the other's soul-spiritual being as in talking to and looking at one another. In the same way that a person's countenance can reflect inner thoughts and feelings, one ought to try to make the physical encounter as clearly expressive as possible of what is going on inwardly.

When you engage in a kiss and think of your next business deal at the same time, the process will be devoid of the kind of qualities which potentially establish closeness. This kind of thing devalues the physical encounter, the quality of tenderness, and the soul is drawn out from the physical happening. Instead the opposite ought to be striven for, namely trying to reach for the other's soul, wondering about him or her, through physical touch. The physical encounter ought to be the continuation of a conversation, something which promotes a soul meeting. Women understand this very well, very much better than men! In marital counselling it becomes very clear that this is exactly what they want. Hence sexuality should be complemented by tenderness and affection, by eroticism, and a more all-encompassing bodily encounter which is at the same time an encounter in soul. In addition there is a whole catalogue of questions in relation to cultivating a relationship in soul and body.

W.W.: A lot of that is covered in our talks on marriage and partnership. Perhaps we could now work on defining the difference between sexuality and love.

W.Gädeke: I would like to refer to Erich Fromm's *The Art of Loving.* He makes clear that love is something different from what is experienced as being-in-love, which drops from the skies like rain and snow. Love is the art of a soul activity in relation to another human being, something that must be acquired by learning. Love does not happen by itself; it is not an ability which we possess in the first place but one we need to acquire through practice. As sexuality is present by force of nature and does not have to be acquired by laborious processes of learning, at least as far as most normal individuals are concerned, it follows of necessity that love and sexuality are two totally different things. I think that if sexuality is not to have these separating effects in a relationship between a woman and man it is important that both partners are really willing to learn the art of loving and to take first steps in the direction outlined by Erich Fromm. If such a will is not present, however tentatively and clumsily it may express itself, the separating component of sexuality will take effect. I recommend Fromm's book for further details of what the art of loving involves.

W.W.: How would you define tender affection and eroticism?

W.Gädeke: Both are adequate expressions of this kind of love.

Perversions of love

W.W.: How about the various forms of sexual one-sidedness? You have already referred to things like the satisfaction of one's sexual drive by means of the other, degradation of the other to a mere object as expressions of excessive antipathy. How about sadism, for example? Is the gesture of affecting the other by way of inflicting pain an excessive form of sympathy in a perverted form?

W.Gädeke: It may be a gesture of sympathy in the sense of overcoming the other, doing something to him, but the gesture of antipathy is once again expressed in the fact that one experiences one's own self in these processes. This is what is so dreadful about it: the experience of self is intensified by humiliating the other. The perversions of love, sadism and masochism, are also described in Fromm's *The Art of Loving.*

W.W.: What is the matter with people who incline towards masochism or sadism?

W.Gädeke: Sadists only experience satisfaction through humiliating others or inflicting pain; this is a clear sign of weakness. If I only experience myself in a full sense by causing pain to another person this is a definite sign of my own weakness and at the same time of my inability to love. The masochistic person only attains a proper experience of self through self-humiliation and self-abandonment; equally a sign of weakness. Unfortunately I do not know whether Rudolf Steiner has said anything about these two perversions of love. However, Erich Fromm writes about these phenomena in a manner so clear and unequivocal that I have not searched any further in Rudolf Steiner's work.

W.W.: Why do you think forms of sexual one-sidedness such as sadism and masochism, but also the use of prostitutes or all the phenomena associated with pornography, are so important in the lives of so many people?

W.Gädeke: It shows that many people are at a great loss in the field of sexuality as a whole. As far as I am concerned these are all symptoms which indicate that people are incapable of integrating sexuality in an all-encompassing relationship between man and woman. This is the stark conclusion to be drawn! The question is, of course, why it is not generally possible to establish sexuality satifactorily into the relationship. In my view this is to do with the fact that female and male sexuality are very different, for if the sexuality of man and woman was naturally compatible there would be no prostitution, everyone would be content with their partner. The fact that many men go to prostitutes demonstrates that there is something here which doesn't quite work. I am not saying that this is the only reason, but it is a very important one.

W.W.: Many men have sexual desires galore, reaching right into the sphere of perversions, they go to prostitutes in order to live them out because they would be ashamed of talking about such things to their wives. Isn't this also a weakness in the ego if one is unable to discuss such problematic issues with one's partner?

W.Gädeke: Of course, but that's not all. In many cases sexual matters will have been discussed endlessly without the problem having been solved. There is increasingly less faith in the possibility of finding understanding in the other. Even if it was possible to discuss absolutely everything, this still doesn't provide any kind of certainty that the emerging problems will be dealt with in the right way. A further reason is that the soul-spiritual realms of our humanness are totally underdeveloped. Everything is one-sidedly fixated on the outer sense-perceptible world; our whole technical civilization with its constant flood of stimuli constantly draws us outward via our senses, and the senses are that which is most physical and body-orientated in us. In other words, our senses today are continually over-stimulated: there is an excessive burden on the one pole of the human being, the nerve/sense organism, whereas the other pole, the metabolic/limb organism remains under-challenged. Male sexuality, in particular, has a lot to do with the limbs, it is in itself a limb function. It could be— and this is my personal conjecture—that our sedentary lifestyle, this movement impoverishment, as it were...

W.W.: ... The typical office worker!

W.Gädeke: ... Yes, exactly... that this inhibition of the natural drive for physical exercise in modern life also contributes to the excessively unbalanced forms of sex. A further cause lies in the fact that throughout modern education the human being is postulated as nothing but a body. It is still the prevailing view of today's materialistic science that the human being is nothing but a physical body. It is considered unscientific to speak of a soul, let alone a spirit. In addition, in line with what Rudolf Steiner called the evolving 'consciousness soul', people are experiencing themselves increasingly strongly as individual beings seeking to grasp the world through intellect and reason. I think that this development of the powers of reason which are needed to understand the world today, is leading to an upsurge of antipathy forces. However, the powers of intellect and reason separate people from others, thereby turning them into objects.

It also needs to be mentioned that our consumer lifestyle leads us more and more to an attitude that the whole world is there for our consumption. The gesture of consumption is a fundamental characteristic of modern man, and as such conducive to considering one's fellow man an object for one's own consumption.

Helpful approaches for the future?

W.W.: Can you identify, for the near future, any helpful approaches towards dealing with sex in the right way, without degenerating into extremes and imbalances? Surely the solution to the problem does not lie in doing without sex altogether and living in asceticism; nor can it be right, I would think, to engage in sexual activity solely for the purpose of procreation or even to limit this to married relationships. On the other hand, it won't be a solution for the future, either, to view sexuality as the ultimate. What's to be done?

W.Gädeke: It is very diffcult, of course. On the one hand we need to be conscious that sexuality always does have something to do with procreation, even though this may not suit us; I already mentioned that this connection is clearly demonstrated by the need to use contraception. It is necessary, in addition, to work out some attitude to the question of children, for it will profoundly affect the sexual union between two partners if one or both of them wish to exclude the possibility of children. We all know the kind of dramas which arise if a child arrives anyway. So, one's attitude to possible offspring is also part of creating the right conditions in the realm of the sexual. Regarding your mention of the Catholic dogma — to practise sex only within marriage — it needs to be said that every dogma contains a grain of truth. After all, we have to confront the fact nowadays that we hardly manage any more to integrate sex satisfactorily into a relationship between two people. Why is that? The question is whether it is possible at all to engage in sex in such a way that the other is not made an object — for nobody wants to be made an object — outside a really sound partnership. I, personally, doubt that this is possible. In my view sex can only be properly integrated into a lasting relationship between two people.

W.W.: But if one doesn't live in such a relationship, then surely one doesn't run the risk of experiencing the alienating quality of sexual relationship, simply because one doesn't live for any length of time with a particular partner.

W.Gädeke: Yes, but this is the very situation where sex is not uniting the people concerned, but separates and degrades them by making them objects.

W.W.: A deeper union is not usually intended anyway!

W.Gädeke: Insofar as this is based on mutual consent things may go well, although one could say a bit more about that. I am thinking of an article by Wilhelm Bittorf in *Spiegel* magazine; allow me to quote from it:

> However, the real reason for the crisis and demise of the instant fuck before AIDS was most probably that in the long run it offended against feelings and desires that nothing in the world can push aside, talk to death or rationalise out of existence. The American writer Erica Jong who, in 1973, sang the praises of casual sex in her bestseller *Fear of Flying* complained eleven years later: 'Many women have discovered that the freedom to say "yes" to everyone may, in reality, be just another form of slavery. Meaningless fleeting encounters in bed did not satisfy their hunger for love or togetherness.'

A few pages later in the same article we may read as follows:

> 'Fury, lust for revenge, fear, discomfort, danger as well as the wish to triumph over all of these — all this became

concentrated in the complex feverish heat that is called sexual arousal', explains Robert J. Stoller, psychoanalyst at the University of California in Los Angeles who has attracted a great deal of attention in recent years. Stoller's theory: In the absence of the un-tender and hostile emotions listed above an intense sexual-erotic experience is not possible at all.

This points in the same direction as my assertion that sexuality entails a paradox, namely that the very opposite of love and affection is inherent in sexuality. Stoller goes on to say:

> During sex each one of the love-entangled partners fights concurrently with his own fears and desires and with his partner, woman and man alike. Even in the case of sex which doesn't look violent from the outside, the forbidden hostile emotions are the crucial ingredient. They are the danger and the risk generated by arousal.

And the feminist Barbara Sichtermann writes in her widely read book *Femininity*:

> It is precisely the women amongst us ... accustomed to expect satisfaction, relaxation, happiness and fun from sex alone – who do not perceive the threat which the fall, the little death ... will also invariably entail for the ego ... A sexual relationship without domination and submission, without lust through pain, is an artifice, quite unthinkable.[4]

These are two more examples which testify to the negative and antipathic aspects of emotion and feeling that are also part of sexuality. And the quote from Erica Jong shows that deeper desires, deeper wishes, deeper feelings remain completely unfulfilled if the relationship between two human beings is just reduced to sex. Hence sexuality in itself is never absolutely satisfying.

W.W.: Our discussion so far has contrasted the contradictory nature of sex with the picture of an ideal form of partnership; but the latter doesn't exist in real life! Most people don't live in such a partnership. Many don't live together with a partner at all. In spite of this, a person who doesn't have a live-in relationship, still has sexual needs and will not want to renounce sex; surely it would not do to advise such a person to exclusively express their sexual needs in an integrated manner within a sound relationship? Taking this realistic situation as a starting point, how does one handle sex nowadays?

W.Gädeke: Let me first respond to this in jocular vein: The emperor Augustus forced his soldiers to marry; the Roman man had to be married and had no excuse, from a certain age onwards, for not having married a woman.

W.W.: Who is emperor Augustus today?

W.Gädeke: No one, of course, such things are out of the question today. This is just one example which shows us that we cannot solve the problem any more. This means, in turn, that one needs to take detours, as it were, which are not fully compatible with what is human; in other words, sexuality has to be instrumentalized in some way, or others have to be used as objects. That means that there is no solution! Of course, this impasse can serve as a new motive for formulating the idea of marriage in a new way, and for making sexuality more human; it may become a reason to decide to live in marriage with a partner.

Of course this doesn't do away with all the other reasons I have stated in our conversation about marriage and partnership; but it would be a thoroughly worthwhile motive—if one has fully realized that sexuality always bears the risk of becoming disassociated, that it is inherently contradictory, and that it bears within it the risk of oppressing the other, of using him as an object. And one might then finally make these reasons a motive for a new impulse, namely for discovering whether it might not be possible to contribute to making sex more human by forming a firm partnership. But you can't then say: Wash me, but don't get me wet! Let me live without a partner, but with a human approach to sex. I can't see this working; it's a contradiction in itself!

W.W.: *Let's take another example: A young person, say 18 years old, lives together with a person of the opposite sex, just as friends; their relationship has existed for some time, they want to stay together but have no wish to become married; but they wish to become sexually involved with each other. What would you advise them, assuming that they asked your advice?*

W.Gädeke: I would talk with them along these lines: the longer the better. But never: You must do this and you mustn't do that! I would say to them: The longer you manage to keep sex out of your relationship altogether, the more free you will be for completing your adolescence and the more free you will be with regard to your choice of partner for the more distant future. This has nothing to do with prudish dogmatism, and is not intended to imply that sex before marriage is bad, but is solely connected with the fact that a young couple of 18 years would, in the other case, be burdening one another with problems with which neither would be fully equipped to cope. Of course I cannot prevent them from starting a sexual relationship – I wouldn't want to, either – but I can tell them: the longer you manage to keep sex out of your relationship, the longer you succeed in confining your physical relationship to kissing and cuddling and the more you fashion your relationship out of the soul and spiritual realms, the better the prospects for your development in the future.

Of course most young people, confronted with this message, would not adhere to it nor would they want to. But when someone actually asks, he is most probably open to such general explanations as I have often given in my marriage courses for young people. It is of course also important to recognize that sexuality is likely to turn into something overpowering if it is completely kept out. That's why it needs to be embedded in the overall questions of life, for then it can be coped with. To what extent two people can live together in such a way that they primarily develop the soul-spiritual side whilst managing to restrict the physical side largely to eroticism and in doing so experience something of an all-encompassing affection — that must be left to their destiny. I am neither able nor willing to hover over them as a watchdog. But I am able to point out to them the problematic nature of sexuality in itself. In other words, I would try to put them in the picture about the paradoxical nature of sex.

W.W.: Some people are of the view that sex is an expression of self-realization and can serve as a means of expressing one's personality in a fuller way. Can you see some justification for such a view or does it point in a totally wrong direction?

W.Gädeke: Self-realization is the realization of the individuality, of the ego. That is why I consider this an aberration of thinking of the highest order, for sexuality is the exact opposite of that which is individual; it is that which is generic, which is related to the species. We have it in common not only with the whole species of man, but also with the animals. It is actually the most 'un-individual' thing about us. Therefore sexuality is not part of our personality or our self, and most certainly not a means of developing that personality. Instead, it is a part of our nature which we have in common with the animal and which we have not yet made human. For if we had already made sexuality human there would be no problems and aberrations in this field, there would be no sado-masochism, no instrumentalization, no prostitution, no exploitation, no degradation of the other human being to an object. All of this represents something which has not been made human, on the contrary, it impedes the impulse to make it human and must first be made human!

W.W.: Will sexuality always exist in the form it manifests today, or will it be transformed in the not too distant future?

W.Gädeke: Rudolf Steiner indicated that sexuality in relation to procreation will be different in a few millennia's time; that infertility would increase. This can already be observed today. In the so-called civilized countries men and women are becoming increasingly infertile. If procreation as we know it today ceased altogether, it cannot be inferred by any means that sexuality would disappear, be overcome in the process, for sexuality in terms of desire is already now almost totally detached from procreation, in stark contrast to the animal world, where the two are still largely connected. The sense of desiring another human being would not be overcome at all. But there are other statements of Rudolf Steiner which make clear that this whole realm which has, since the division of humanity into the female and the male, led to very specific stages of evolution, this attraction between the sexes, will one day be superseded, be overcome as a natural part of the further evolution of the earth. However, only if we, as human beings, support this process.

2. Partnership – Does Lifelong Monogamy Make Sense?

Wolfgang Weirauch: Considering the fact that well over fifty per cent of the marriages entered into in the last ten years have been dissolved the question arises whether lifelong monogamy is actually an institution that makes sense.

Wolfgang Gädeke: If a teacher gives his class a test and over fifty per cent of the students get very bad results one would assume for certain that it is not the pupils who are to blame but the teacher who prepared them badly for the task. He has asked too much of them.

If the failure rate of marriages is around fifty per cent – although probably it is much higher, there are estimates that it is up to eighty per cent, depending on cultural and social background – then one must simply ask oneself the question whether lifelong monogamy makes any sense whatsoever. Who for example actually still expects this?

W.W.: Let's formulate the idea of a marriage as follows: a lifelong monogamous relationship with one partner on a spiritual, soul and physical level. Does this concept of marriage which is, after all, the one held today, relate to one that was previously held in the past?

W. Gädeke: It may be surprising for some to hear that this idea of marriage has not always been so and that lifelong monogamy has not always been taken for granted in this way. Indeed, this old unquestioned concept of marriage must first of all be radically called into question. Even though a lot of people today are doing just that existentially, it ought to be done much more clearly and consciously. For many people still regard it as natural to get married, i.e. in our terms: to live permanently with one partner of the opposite gender in a confined space.

Types of marriage in the animal kingdom

W.W.: *Are there marriage-type relationships in the animal kingdom? And what form do they take?*
W. Gädeke: As we know, in the animal kingdom every species has its own specific form of sexual cohabitation. Every possible form exists, for example the monogamous stork as well as the bigamous baboon. Furthermore there is the stag who lives with a whole herd of does. Some spiders eat up their husbands right after the wedding. Amongst the bees one female is the centre of a whole state, the drones are driven away after the wedding and perish. Many more examples could be given. All possible forms of cohabitation are conceivable and appear in the animal world, but each is determined by the species.

Types of marriage in ancient cultures

W.W.: *Has the idea of lifelong monogamy hitherto not existed within any single culture?*
W. Gädeke.: First of all it needs to be emphasized that our human nature does not predetermine us to this form of monogamy for life. A human being's natural instincts do not compel him to this type of cohabitation between the sexes, and therefore marriage has never been a fact of *nature* but a question of *culture*. In all cultures there have been different forms of marriage, but of a widely divergent nature: polygamy, serial marriage, group marriage, monogamy. Marriages have existed in which a woman had several husbands or a man several wives. Even today these forms can still be found in certain cultures. There was also the specific form of monogamy during very early stages of civilization, yet only as one amongst many forms of marriage.

However, the so-called promiscuity — in other words the

state of utter lack of form in this realm which was once attributed to earlier times — was not found to have existed in the old stone age cultures which were discovered as late as this century. Whilst it is true that there were in those times forms of group marriage which from the outside looked as if promiscuity prevailed, there was never a complete lack of form in this realm.

That proves that in all human cultures there was always some form of marriage which would have been enforced by all possible sanctions, but it was never exclusively *one* form. There is also no such thing as an evolution from promiscuity to group marriage and polygamy and finally monogamy. The history of civilization does not admit of such a reading.

Marriage in the Old and New Testament

W.W.: How about the Bible? Is there no mention in either the Old or the New Testament about lifelong monogamy, as we defined it, say in St. Paul, for example.

W. Gädeke: This may sound shocking to some, but there is simply no imperative to monogamy in the Old Testament. Quite the opposite, there are many great personalities and leaders who had many wives as a matter of fact. The Hebrew culture was patriarchal, and it was a matter of course that Abraham, for example, had a 'maid' besides his wife. Also Jacob, Israel, who gave the whole people its name, had two wives as well as two maids and it was a matter of course that the maids' children enjoyed equal status and rights. David had many wives, Solomon even had a whole harem. So monogamy was not assumed in the Old Testament.

Even in the New Testament only marriage is referred to initially, not monogamy. There is only one exception, and that is in Timothy's letter in the New Testament, in which

Paul requires of the Bishop that he should be the husband of one woman only. Therefore one must really ask oneself what marriage means in terms of the Bible.

W.W.: Does this passage in Paul imply that the Bishop have one woman for all spiritual, soul and physical needs or could it also mean that the Bishop should have one wife for spiritual companionship, but additional ones for sex?

W. Gädeke: That is probably out of the question in this case. However, throughout the entire era of Western Christianity's existence — right up to the sixteenth century — concubinage was a perfectly acceptable and legal principle. Only in the sixteenth century was monogamy laid down as the only legally valid form of marriage. But as far as Paul is concerned I think it's fair to say that only one woman is referred to in this passage: however, this monogamy is only expected from the Bishop.

W.W.: From the point of view of Christian theology marriage is bestowed upon people by God, namely through Eve having been created out of Adam's rib to be his wife. Can one see it in that way?

W. Gädeke: It is problematic to interpret the words spoken by the God Jahve after the separation of the genders, as represented in the Old Testament, as the bestowal of marriage. All that is said there is that the man would leave father and mother, that he would be attached to his wife and that they would become one flesh.

A far better way of understanding this sentence is to interpret it in terms of the natural instinctual attraction between the sexes which arises out of the fact that two different human bodies and human beings evolved from the archetype. I would be more inclined to interpret this sentence as a prophesy, as something giving expression to the instinctual drive that has arisen between the sexes as a result of the differentiation of the genders, and not as a commandment, let alone a bestowal of a cultural form, but simply as a description of a natural drive. So it can simply not be said that the meaning of marriage in our time can be derived from that, as there can be no doubt whatsoever about the existence of an instinctual drive between man and woman.

Children as the reason for marriage?

W.W.: *If we continue our search for the reason or meaning of a marriage to one person for life, inevitably the question of children arises. Are children, their birth and raising a reason for lifelong marriage?*

W. Gädeke: It is common for cohabiting couples to get married when a child is expected. Usually the argument is that the children should grow up in a proper family. But this is extremely problematic, as modern sociological research provides us with ample evidence that a family marriage — that is a woman, a man and their children — can fundamentally only be conducted in a healthy and right manner when it is supported by an intact marriage between the adult partners. In other words, if the marriage partnership between two people of the opposite sex lacks an inherent meaning and purpose, it will not be able to support children, and making the latter the sole purpose of marriage is tantamount to burdening and misusing them. Children must be presented with an intact marital relationship which derives its meaning from within itself. Only then will they be able to flourish within that marriage, but not the other way round.

At most, the fact that there are children might act as a prompt to think seriously about the continuation of the partnership in question but they are not the basis and the meaning of a lifelong monogamous marriage.

W.W.: *If the children did provide the sole meaning of a marriage, presumably the marriage would be devoid of meaning when the children had left home, at the latest?*

W. Gädeke: In that case the marriage would be a marriage with a deadline, for example until the children are of age, and would then have fulfilled its purpose.

Love or being in love?

W.W.: How about love? One loves another like no one else in the world, and that is to be the reason for marrying. Is that enough?
W. Gädeke: Well, first of all one needs to ask oneself what love actually is. That which first occurs in human life, quite naturally, and is called love, should really be described as 'being in love'. This state of being in love happens all by itself; no one can predict it, no one can direct it. The fact that one slips suddenly into 'love' is a natural phenomenon. The English call it 'falling in love'.

Since falling in love is a natural event it cannot be a cultural event. And it is common knowledge today that the state of being in love vanishes as quickly as it arises. The condition of 'in-loveness' lasts for two years at the most. This has also been empirically proven by now. A relationship for life cannot be built on this. So when a couple states: We are building our partnership for life on love, then all one can say is: 'Fine, never mind, it will pass!' But being in love is certainly no basis for a marriage.

W.W.: If there is nothing in the past to support the conventional idea of marriage, and if there is no other way to invest it with more purpose and meaning, then one could actually say that all the people married today have entered into that state with no purpose whatsoever and could – to put it drastically – actually marry several partners at the same time. Could one put it like that?
W. Gädeke: Yes, the facts of everyday life today serve to make this quite clear. It's in fact the main reason for the great number of divorces and difficulties in this area. People aim at something, namely sharing their life with a person of the opposite sex, without knowing why they should really do so or want to do so. It is not possible to give

form to something that is not a natural phenomenon and must be a cultural deed when it is not known where it should lead and why it should be lived at all.

Similarly I wouldn't dream of building or designing a machine before establishing whether I want to travel in it by sea, land or air. I would need to know beforehand what is to become of my plans. What we want to accomplish and work through in terms of culture must not be devoid of meaning and purpose. And if meaning and purpose of lifelong monogamy are not even thinkable, how could they possibly be lived?

W.W.: *Are you saying that the institution of marriage is something propped up by convention whilst utterly devoid of meaning?*

W. Gädeke: Marriage today is devoid of meaning. In earlier times it had a meaning. But in the past the concept of marriage did not live as an individual concept in each single person, but was predetermined from outside as a social form to which the individual was expected to conform. That worked to an extent, but today people can no longer live together in this way. The only way of living today is knowing what you are doing and why you are doing it. Today many marriages fail because the individual's striving for freedom and self-determination is so strong that it is no longer accepted that an institution — state or church — should dictate how or why one should live together with members of the opposite sex.

Biological and soul differences between man and woman

W.W.: *Male-dominated society has ascribed rather different roles in marriage to man and woman, roughly in the following pattern: the man is responsible for work, he is strong, clear and sober, with an objective outlook. The woman in turn is a born mother and birth apparatus, her place is in the kitchen and she is weak, sensitive and emotional. Does such a categorization hold true?*

W. Gädeke: Of course it is especially the women who rightly oppose this kind of categorization because it has been used to justify a lot of oppression, inequality and favouring of the man in the past and of course this can and must not be perpetuated. However, this does not mean that there is no difference between man and woman. But what happened to begin with in the movement against this old role pattern is that the baby was thrown out with the bath water and it was considered the highest aim of emancipation that women should do all that a man does. Fortunately even in the women's movement these things have come to be reconsidered, so that it is no longer put forward as an objective to become like men in all respects. After all, equality need not mean that one has to be and do the same thing, since equality in terms of rights is something very different from 'being of the same kind' — and there is absolutely no way one could say that men and women are of the same kind. But equality in terms of rights must be striven for.

W.W.: If one assumes that woman and man are not simply interchangeable it is surely possible to deduce certain characteristic features typical to each gender? What would be the typical characteristics of the male and the female?

W.Gädeke: One of the simplest descriptions of biology is for example that the male is physically larger and heavier. If we interpret this it means that the male is more strongly related to the earth. He is more strongly permeated with the element of earth. It follows from that that he is more 'dead' in his constitution than the woman. It is not only that he cannot bring forth any children, but also his life expectancy is about ten per cent lower. Already *in utero* there are 100 female embryos to 130 male ones. But there are 106 male births to 100 female ones.

W.W.: Does that mean that male mortality in utero is higher?

W.Gädeke: Male mortality is very much higher. In addition, the so-called perinatal mortality rate, i.e. the number of baby deaths around birth, is higher for boys than girls. It is also a fact acknowledged by sociologists and psychologists today that the various developmental stages are accompanied by greater difficulties in boys than in girls, not only that of puberty but also all the other crisis-like changes in development, and that in all problem groups, such as dyslexics and children with behavioural anomalies, boys are clearly over-represented. So one can say that the male is inherently further removed from nature, from natural life; he is more 'dead', more problematic in his entire development.

W.W.: Can we contrast this now with what is typically female?
W.Gädeke: She is biologically in a position to bring forth a new human life; not by herself, indeed, but the man's temporal-spatial involvement in this biological process — the fertilization — is really tiny in relation to what pregnancy and nursing represent. In addition, pregnancy is connected with a soul relationship that naturally impinges far deeper on the whole of a woman's life than the soul relationship to procreation does in a man.

Woman is — as is already stated in the Bible about Eve — the Mother of all that is living. She is more strongly connected with life — to the extent that the moon's rhythms determine the monthly rhythm of the woman as long as it comes to pass naturally. This indicates a relationship to the cosmos which a man does not have.

W.W.: Are the physical organs of the male and the female, in particular the sexual organs, indicative of the typical character, the specific soul characteristics of man and woman?
W.Gädeke: The bodies of the male and of the female display relative differences. Whilst it is true that we all have a nose in the middle of our face, a head and limbs, very different forms are created by the different hormonal processes. Of course this is particularly marked in the reproductive organism. Here, too, it must be added that the woman possesses the archetypal organism, because the gonads — as in all embryos — are first situated in the upper region of the

abdominal cavity, and only shortly before or shortly after birth do they descend into the testicular sac in the case of the male, whilst in the female they remain in place.

The entire sexual organization of the man is outwardly disposed and has limb character. In contrast the woman's sexual organization is almost entirely disposed inwards and has metabolic character. Of course both of these variants have a bearing on consciousness. When we are healthy we are asleep in our metabolic life and have no consciousness of what goes on in our metabolism; we only become conscious of metabolic processes when these are affected by illness. On the other hand, as man and woman, we are very conscious of the movements of our limbs. That means, if the man's sexual organism assumes limb character, the man's consciousness of the sexual organism is very much more awake than the woman's.

Likewise the difference between male and female gonads in relation to shape and function is very telling. The female ovary cells are all present at the time of the girl's birth and mature individually in the course of years following puberty, but there is no further cell division in the ovaries. The ovaries are also relatively calm and the eggs have no inherent movement. The exact opposite applies in the man: the testicles display a continuous inherent movement, producing millions of sperm per day. These sperm are not round, spherically shaped and calm but elongated with strong inherent motion.

W.W.: They also have the character of limbs!

W.Gädeke: Yes, that's true. And so one can say from the point of view of biological shape that everything spherical and round is a female formation (head formation), whereas everything linear and straight is a male (limb) formation.

It should also be mentioned that in a woman the sexual organism is more inclined to the middle realm of the human being. This is not only expressed in the words: 'She carries a child under her heart', but also in the fact that her sexual organism is positioned higher than the man's. Metabolic processes connected with the sexual reach right into the chest region, for example in the case of nourishment through the lactic glands. In the man, however, everything sexual inclines away from the middle in a downward direction to the limbs.

Looking at the structure of the man's and the woman's sexual organism one might even say that the ovaries correspond to the testicles, the vagina to the penis. However, the middle organ of the female sexual organism, the uterus—which, as a hollow muscle, is very similar to the heart, right down to its muscular structure—has no correspondence in the middle region of the man's sexual organism.

All this must have its effects on the soul life. What it means to be in a male or a female body simply cannot be grasped by the opposite sex.

W.W.: What typical soul characteristics can be deduced from this physical oppositeness of man and woman?

W.Gädeke: There is a very good book by Ekkehard Kloehn: *Typisch männlich? Typisch weiblich?* ['Typically male? typically female?']. In this book the endeavour is made to view the whole of modern research in biology, psychology and sociology in terms of the difference between man and woman, differentiating clearly between biological differences and differences as a result of upbringing, social conditions, role expectations etc.

The view according to which all soul-related differences between man and woman are merely a consequence of upbringing is no longer tenable. Whilst it is true that human nature is malleable it is not possible to bring about something so opposite through upbringing. For example, boys clearly have a stronger orientation to spatial consciousness in their conceptual life whereas girls have a stronger picture consciousness and sensitivity to language. Boys incline more towards concentration and orientation through the eye, optical perception; girls towards perceiving through the sense of touch, tactile perception.

This book also lists a whole number of things which are so firmly anchored in the biological structure that no formative influences through upbringing could possibly make them disappear, let alone produce them. Another example is that boys incline far more strongly to games of a risk and fighting nature than girls, that they tend very much more strongly towards playing in groups and engaging in competitive patterns within those. Girls, in turn, have a far stronger tendency to have just one special friend. They are also more inclined to making arrangements and distributing roles — in other words, to developing a kind of legal form in the social life.

One simply has to conclude: The biological difference gives rise to certain basic patterns in the difference of soul life even though the latter will not manifest as absolutely as the biological differences.

The difference between man and woman — the anthroposophical perspective

W.W.: What about the anthroposophical perspective of the difference between man and woman? Which constituent members of the human being are specific to gender?

W.Gädeke: The anthroposophical conception of the human being encompasses a number of fundamental and important ideas concerning the difference between man and woman. The human being as spirit, his personality, his ego, are of course neither male nor female. In contrast we have seen that the body is unequivocally male or female. All else that exists between the human spirit (the individuality) and the human body — i.e. the human life forces which build and sustain the physical-material body, and the soul forces which mediate between the animated body and the spirit—is difficult to categorize in terms of female and male.

The spirit is completely devoid of gender, the concept of gender makes no sense at all in relation to the spirit, but it makes *absolute* sense in relation to the body. In between—in the life and soul realm—there are transitions between the two.

Rudolf Steiner said that the man's life forces are female and the woman's male. Maybe this is more clearly illustrated if one considers that it is the life forces which build up the physical body. Assuming that these life forces in their entirety are originally male and female—in the man as well as in the woman—it might be plausible that the male life forces so exert themselves in the building of a male body, in this great emphasis on the limb character, and that the female life forces, which would be in a position to form female physical organs, do not work in an organ-building capacity in the male.

The reverse would apply to woman: The female life forces create the female organs, and the male life forces simply don't need to come into effect.

We must also consider another important finding from anthroposophy, and that is that the life forces which are never or no longer needed in building up the body, are thus available to the conscious life of soul, to learning etc. That means that the woman has male life forces at the disposal of her conscious soul life and the man female ones.

W.W.: *What characterizes a female and male etheric body, respectively?*

W.Gädeke: The etheric forces which are not required for building organs in the reproductive system, i.e. the man's female life forces, for example, are available to his conscious life of soul, predominantly his conceptual and thinking life; that means that in the very place where we are built in a female way, spherically—in our head formation—the place where we are receptive to thoughts and perceptions, there is, in the man, an additional female quality — a receptive quality. As a result the man is biologically predestined to become objective to the point of fanaticism, in that he really only receives what comes in, leaving well alone what has thus been received. He develops a science that is totally based on objectivity. All he wants is to let the world speak, not himself, neither his own imagination nor his feelings, but only that which comes from outside.

What results from this among other things is that men very often get upset at women because they think completely differently, for in the conscious soul portion of their thinking and concept-forming women will always have a certain proportion of inherent life, no matter whether this manifests as desire or imagination. Women are never so keen to ask what the world in itself represents, but they ask what the world is to them personally and how it might be changed. This gives expression to an element of will, a male element which is derived from that portion of male life forces which were not involved in building organs and are thus available to the conscious life of soul.

W.W.: What about the constitutional characteristics of homosexual men or lesbian women?

W.Gädeke: Concerning people who feel an inner desire to live together with persons of their own gender, there are, as we know, many variations. There are those who are not unequivocally male or female with regard to the physical body. Then there are those who in their social conditioning, in early childhood, were not raised in accordance with their biological gender.

It is a good thing that it is possible today to consider the problem of 'homophilia', to use a more appropriate term, unemotionally and separate from moral considerations. This makes it possible, for example, to identify the phenomenon that male homophilics are far less capable of commitment and tend to have a greater number of different partners. This was an important issue in the discussions around AIDS. With regard to women it may be observed that lesbian women are much more inclined to commit themselves to one partner, they tend to be involved with the same partner far longer than homophilic men and also show a far greater inclination to cultivate their relationship beyond the physical, whereas homophilic men easily slip into a state where they are constantly on the chase, perpetually looking for new and different partners. These phenomena indicate that homophilia manifests differently in men and women.

W.W.: Can it be concluded that homophilic men also have a male ether body and that lesbian women have a female ether body?

W.Gädeke: This thought might be entertained once and then left open as a fruitful question, but I would not assert such a thing. I am also not aware of any indication of Rudolf Steiner in this direction, but maybe it is a solution to this question.

Division of the sexes

W.W.: What is the division of the sexes according to Rudolf Steiner's indications? What happened in those distant times?

W. Gädeke: Looking at natural, biological evolution it is quite clear that all the original forms of life — in the realm of plant and animal alike — are genderless in the sense that procreation is performed by plant and animal individuals that are not separated into male or female. The differentiation of male and female is not necessarily connected with the continuation of life. That this might have also applied to the human being is made probable by the fact that one may clearly identify an early stage in the germinal development of the human being in which, with regard to the forms and functions of the fertilized ovum and the growing embryo there is no difference between the male and the female apart from the difference in chromosomes.

This only affects the growing form at a later stage, so that a male or female embryo develops.

So one might wonder whether there could have been primeval states of human existence where the male and female were still undifferentiated. Whilst it is not possible to prove this in an external scientific manner at present it is true that all religions and myths point to such a possibility. A famous example is Plato's spherical human in the dialogue *Symposion*. In the Old Testament, too, the human being is referred to as being created male-female as an image of God. Adam in paradise must not be envisaged as a man, he is merely called 'the earthen one', the one made out of earth. The division of the genders is represented in the Old Testament by Jahve taking a rib out of Adam and creating out of that a second human being, a woman, and only through that does Adam become a man.

So there are indications in practically all religions and myths that the human being was not originally a man or a woman but a higher unity of both. This thought proves to be extraordinarily fruitful and it is not contradicted by the biological facts. Out of his spiritual science Rudolf Steiner speaks unequivocally about the event of the division of the genders which took place at a definite time of early earth evolution, and as a result of which the act of procreation which until then was accomplished by a single individual became divided up between two different individuals.

W.W.: The consequences of the division of the sexes are that evil was enabled to find a way in. In the Christmas Plays from Oberufer *Lucifer is called the 'marriage devil'.*

W.Gädeke: The division of genders had very varied consequences. On the positive side it has made it possible for a part of the individual human being's life force no longer to have to serve the purpose of procreation, thus becoming available to the higher and conscious forces of soul. In this light we may understand Rudolf Steiner saying that the division of the genders was a prerequisite for the brain's development into an organ of conscious thinking activity. It would be difficult to interpret this in any other fashion. After all, what made it possible, all of a sudden, that such a highly developed central nervous system could be developed?

Another consequence is, for example, that on the level of instinctual drive the fundamental conditions are given for that which can manifest in its highest form as human love; this is based on the natural attraction between the genders and in the consequent soul-physical process between the genders. On the negative side one could say that as a result of the division of the genders the human being is faced with something strange in the other, who is like him in one sense, and not like him in another. Many people today suffer a lot from these opposites of man and woman, women more so than men. But it is understandable that there is a desire to understand one another better and more easily, rather than embarking on a war between the sexes.

Problems in communication and marriage crises

W.W.: The one-sided nature of both sexes gives rises to commu-nication problems between people; in friendships, relationships and in marriage. Are there certain characteristic problems between man and woman?
W.Gädeke: In the first place we are probably all inclined to naively believe that the other thinks and feels as I do. Yet it forms part of married people's painful experience that this is absolutely not the case. It becomes easier to understand the reasons for this if one studies the phenomenon of the division of the sexes and its consequences, be it in the context of anthroposophical spiritual science or with the help of Ekkehard Kloehn's book. In any case one will acquire some understanding of the state of affairs as it undeniably is. This is an absolutely basic pre-condition for

any inquiry about how men and women might get along with one another. In the absence of a clear recognition that men and women typically have certain characteristic differences, there is little hope of finding ways of fruitful co-existence.

W.W.: *Are the problems between man and woman, within marriage or outside of it, individual problems or are there certain recurrent types or conglomerates of problems?*

W.Gädeke: Most of the problems between men and women, married or unmarried, are typical, i.e. not individual, because as individuals we are not man and woman. It is in those very areas where we are generically determined — either male or female — that the problems occur as a direct consequence of the difference between the genders.

In the realm of the spiritual, for example in mathematics, there can be no male-female differences. Three times three equals nine, and not ten or eight. It makes no sense at all to speak of gender-specific mathematics, even if it should be proven that mathematics as such is somewhat easier for the male brain to grasp than it is for the female. In spite of that, mathematics is neither male nor female; it merely holds true that the brain can be more or less suited to grasp its contents.

W.W.: *Can you say more about typical marriage problems?*

W. Gädeke: The first basic problem we have already referred to has to to with the fact that partners in marriage need to do something of which most of them have not even a theoretical understanding: to conduct the marriage.

The second problem is that most people are not able to distinguish between the naturally determined difference between the sexes and that which they desire to overcome. There is a very common view that men and women should get on fine, because all the basic work to make that possible has been done.

A further problem is that we are not prepared in any way for marriage, there is no training for acquiring the capacity for conducting a marriage, in spite of the fact that every cultural deed of the human being presupposes some form of training. In actual fact there ought to be three to four year courses in marriage preparation and study to do justice to the enormous significance of man and woman living toge-ther. Just as only a few centuries ago it was held that pedagogy was not something one had to learn about, and today it is the subject of whole sciences and training cour-ses. I am convinced that it will not be very long before men and women will undergo some training before they marry — and as this is not happening yet problems are bound to arise.

The concept of marriage

W.W.: *Who was the first to bring up the concept of life-long monogamy in the realms of body, soul and spirit?*
W.Gädeke: In most of the cultures of the past the commu-nity between man and woman was confined to specific areas of life. The Roman *domina*, the mistress of the house, for example, was the undisputed ruler over everything within the house, she commanded the slaves and was the mother of the children who were entitled to inherit, but she did not have to be the mistress, neither did she have to be the one with whom her husband conducted intelligent conversation or any other exchange of that nature. The Japanese had the *geishas* who were more than simple prostitutes as they were highly educated in the arts and sciences; and the Greeks had the *hetairas*. There was no claim on the wife for any exchange in spirit and soul.

The community of the sexes on a physical, soul and spiritual level was separated out, as it were — and the ideal of a fruitful togetherness in all areas of human existence with one partner only emerged during the era of German Romanticism. The romantics — Schlegel, Tieck, Brentano, etc. — had this ideal. They also had great women with whom they tried to live out this ideal; Karoline Schelling, for example. However, they all failed this ideal to a greater or lesser extent, but we ought not to reproach them with that. They were the first to conceive of it — and it is not surprising that, after centuries of other forms of marriage, the representatives of this new idea of marriage were not immediately able to make it a living reality. It's important to remember that this all-encompassing idea of marriage is not even two hundred years old.

W.W.: *If the raison d'être for life-long monogamy is not to be found in the past then the idea of marriage must be conceived anew if marriage is to be instilled with meaning. What are the components of a new, meaningful marriage idea?*

W.Gädeke: The idea of marriage is something that needs to be conceived completely afresh and cannot simply be described in one sentence. One part of it certainly would be that life-long monogamy must be regarded as something to be created by human work and human effort.

One component of this something we call marriage is the task of learning true love in life. This does not mean love in the sense we discussed earlier, i.e. being in love as a fact of nature, but love in the sense of having a capacity, an ability. Fundamental to that is Erich Fromm's book *The Art of Loving*. Whoever is not willing to acquire the ability to love in the terms described there, and indeed for an entire lifetime, needn't even begin today to consider conducting a marriage as an enduring life partnership. It cannot work. This idea of love must become a personal ideal. It must become an ideal to want to learn this art, to want to learn something that the human being is not able to do by nature. All nature does is make it possible to fall in love. But love as a skill that is consciously grasped and practised in terms of how Erich Fromm talks about it, with all its constituent parts in theory and practice — that is something I have to carry within myself as an ideal, and I must be so strongly imbued with this ideal that I abandon my Self if I abandon this ideal. This ideal has to become part of my own ego, for me and for my partner. This belongs to the concept of marriage.

W.W.: *What else belongs to it?*

W.Gädeke: Something which can be derived from the different natures of man and woman we talked about earlier. Once you have actually acknowledged how male or female you really are, and to what extent certain behaviours and ways of feeling are fixed and determined—right into the soul realm—then this realization may give rise to a longing to overcome this one-sidedness by appreciating and loving another human being because he or she is of a different nature. It would be wrong to love him or her for reinforcing one's own one-sidedness as this only creates dependence. One would rather try to love in such a way that one can say to oneself: I want to consciously learn and practise that which the other has by virtue of nature and destiny as man or woman; I will at least try to embark on this path.

If you pay attention to these things you will find that certain abilities inherent in the woman are very much more helpful in certain situations than those a man has by virtue of his maleness. Ekkehard Kloehn gives excellent examples of how man and woman can learn from each other; there are of course other situations in life where the natural male response is more helpful and appropriate.

When one has succeeded in acknowledging one's own one-sidedness, the way one is tied to the generic destiny of being male or female, the ideal can arise—and that is more than a mere longing—to embark on a conscious path together with one's partner to try and overcome, as far as possible, the differences, the onesidedness, which have come into the world as a result of the separation of the sexes, and also to learn about what the other has, and oneself lacks.

However, such efforts should not be confined to the

conscious area of the soul life: they must be extended right into the realm of the life forces. Whilst it is of course possible to strive for this ideal in relation to a friend of the other sex whom one meets from time to time, the real, deeper differences—down to the realm of habit etc. can only be learned about in context with a partner with whom I share my life on a more permanent basis. This is why in earlier times marriage was always understood to be a community of table and bed, of eating and sleeping, the fundamental facts of life. To have community in those areas, not only in the realm of soul and spirit, but especially in the realm of the life forces—that is marriage.

Marriage as a cultural deed

W.W.: Does marriage as the archetypal cell of human community also have a significance for human culture in its entirety?
W.Gädeke: Indeed this is also part of the concept of marriage! In the past it has always been the prevailing pattern that individuals and groups of people settled their conflicts by either making war with one another, declaring enmities or killing one another—or else by parting company altogether. It makes no difference whether we think of England's penal colony in Australia or the central European bourgeois way of pushing deviant sons out to America— problems were always solved by going somewhere different. Solving problems by going away or engaging in battle!

Problems between man and woman also give rise to this kind of approach: either there is war and the parties engage in battle or else they take leave of one another. It's the same basic pattern. All problems between people arise as a result of difference or disagreement—be it the apartheid problem in South Africa, different religions, world views or political systems—it is always the differences that give rise to problems. However, our civilization clearly shows us that these old approaches to problem solving — parting ways or engaging in battle — are no longer fruitful today. War is not a means of solving problems. Parting ways is no longer possible either, in view of the restricted space on our planet. The ancient conflict-settling strategies no longer work.

One of the deepest problems, that of the most fundamental differences between human beings — deeper than race, nation or language — is the difference between man and woman. I can take hold of this difference as my personal problem. However, I do not aim even to attempt to resolve this difference between man and woman by resorting to any of the old strategies — taking leave or engaging in battle. Instead I will try and solve this fundamental problem of humanity from which we are all suffering today, as we have not yet developed a new strategy for conflict resolution, by putting my own individual will behind it. I will begin in my own closest environment to live in community with that wholly other human being. I will not just succumb to this inevitability and suffer it passively; I will rather embrace it consciously; for this reason I decide to live in lifelong monogamy. In that way I exercise something, within the smallest possible circle, that mankind urgently needs for its survival. It is thus possible to say that the decision to live in lifelong monogamy can contribute towards solving a problem which is worldwide and concerns the whole of humanity.

W.W.: *In the context of this approach to conducting a marriage I can also try and learn to sit around a table with a group of other people for the sake of one shared aim or ideal, even though there may be great differences between the people, or even hostilities.*

W.Gädeke: The difficulty and the illusion of the last twenty years has been that in many strata of society people became aware of the problematic nature of the traditional marriage and small family, and this led some to orientate themselves towards living in communes, cohabiting communities and other larger scale communal settings. But it is an illusion to think that such changes would make it easier to overcome the differences. Practical experience clearly shows that it doesn't get easier but rather more difficult the more single individuals participate and the more complex the web of relationships becomes.

W.W.: *But I am not thinking now of communes and other forms of communal living, but of people who share anthroposophy as a higher ideal and are incapable, due to the differences in view otherwise, to sit around one table. Is this because they have not yet consciously taken this ideal on board?*

W.Gädeke: Yes, because on the one hand they have not truly understood what separates them and on the other they haven't yet grasped what their shared ideal, the common direction of their will, really is. However, when this has not been learnt and practised in small contexts—neither in theory nor in practice—it can't be expected to happen of its own accord in larger contexts, not in the case of anthroposophists either; it simply won't work!

'True love never ends'

W.W.: *Let's resume the subject of love once more. It is often stated that love is of limited duration. Can the kind of love of which you spoke be invested in two different people during one human life, for example?*

W.Gädeke: When you really think through this idea of love as an art as developed by Fromm, you get to a point where you say to yourself like St Paul that, if it is real love, it can never cease. For if it does cease you can be sure that it was not love. Love is undividable. I cannot love a human being in the higher sense if I love him for certain characteristics: because he is young, beautiful or strong, because he has lovely blue eyes, because he is especially witty, or because he is affectionate or for any other features in his soul or bodily nature. If I love him or her for any of those things I do not truly love because it is not the whole human being that I love. Love is only present when it extends to the whole of a human being, in body, soul and spirit.

However, the decisive thing is that I do not just love the other as she or he is now, but also as a temporal being, a biography. We are, after all, not complete at any given moment: we are only wholly ourselves in the context of our entire life. For that reason I can only really say that I truly love a human being – that I have mastered this art – when I have loved him for an entire lifetime. Thus the concept of true love as evolved by Fromm necessarily implies a duration for life. The fact that this kind of love may then gradually be extended to other people as well is a different matter altogether.

W.W.: And insofar as love is actually not undividable?

W. Gädeke: Insofar it is not exclusive! Once I have learnt the art of truly loving I can begin to extend this to other people, too.

The more free the decision to marry the healthier the marriage

W.W.: Is marriage also a free deed or could there be – anthroposophically speaking – karmic reasons for marrying particular people?

W.Gädeke: Maybe it happened in the past that marriage was derived from destiny-related connections. But even in earlier times, in almost all cultures, more or less importance was attached to both partners freely agreeing to a marriage even if it was determined by parents or others. This freedom was not very wide in terms of how we define it today, but nevertheless there was an expectation that it should happen voluntarily. This goes to show that even in the distant past people had at least a feeling kind of consciousness that marriages should not be concluded out of some necessities of the past. This applies all the more today when there is a wish to conduct a marriage and when this is derived from an idea in accordance with which one strives to live, for marriage is a task for the future.

The more people decide on a life together without looking for reasons rooted in the past and the more they develop goals for the future towards which they strive, the more healthy their life together will be. The soundness of a marriage is directly related to the measure of freedom entailed in the decision to marry and to the absence of any reasoning related to karmic, destiny-related past connections.

In primeval times it was customary to marry the people to whom one was related, with whom one was connected by nature anyway. This form of sibling marriage had to be substituted by marriage between unrelated individuals, and that means a lower degree of relatedness in destiny, too. According to something Rudolf Steiner once said in conversation it will not even be particularly fortuitous in the future to marry someone to whom one was closely connected in a previous life—as siblings or marriage partners. The lesser the connection from the past and the freer the decision to marry, the better the chances for that life together to be successful.

W.W.: So marriages are not made in heaven?

W.Gädeke: At least not by others and not by predestination, either; for heaven must be found on earth by raising oneself up to the ideal. The marriage can be 'made in heaven' when one truly raises oneself up to an idea, seeking more than the need to live together comfortably and being nice and kind to one another in order to satisfy one another's physical and soul needs.

W.W.: In other words, is the 'great karmic encounter' on account of which one files for a divorce in order to marry the new partner nothing but wishful thinking, egotistic sham reasoning, anthroposophically packaged?

W.Gädeke: An encounter with a person of the opposite sex may very well be a grandiose fact of destiny, determined from the past, which comes to pass of necessity and can be of an overwhelming quality. Very often it is a case of being-in-love, but all this is no reason for marrying. One has to simply differentiate there, for it is certainly not pre-destined how and in what way one shapes and lives out the destiny of that encounter; this is not determined by past destiny but must be done out of freedom.

Preparation for marriage

W.W.: How can one prepare for marriage?
W.Gädeke: The preparation is related to what we have discussed already and consists in forming very clear pictures about the essential nature of the two genders as well as the differences between man and woman. As in Waldorf pedagogy which is based on a very specific study of the human being, such as the various seven-year-stages from the birth of the child to its maturity, and which requires on-going work and research for a better and better understanding of its principles, so the human facts underlying two people's life together equally require constant study.

A further requirement is that one should ask oneself why one wishes to get married in the first place. Thirdly it is important to attain a certain maturity for marriage, i.e. to be quite capable of living on one's own, for example, and to have lived through the process of individuation in the fourth seven-year-cycle to the extent that one may be certain that one could cope with life on one's own. That implies earning your own money, managing life out of your own resources, not needing the other for a crutch to your existence. For marriage is, after all, an additional task in life and not an institution for solving problems. Once you make all of this clear to yourself you understand that it is an excellent thing to know that you could survive on your own if need be. To put it in a fairly extreme way, one could say that we're ready for marriage if we can do without it!

The civil wedding

W.W.: *What purpose does a marriage in a registry office have?*

W.Gädeke: The registry office marriage has, of course, no relevance with regard to the course of the marriage, its foundations and its stability; fortunately all it does is provide for certain legal and financial consequences in case the marriage should fail — in the event of a divorce. German marital legislation is fairly progressive in the sense that it no longer defines the marriage's content but merely describes the outer fact of a marriage. In a registry office wedding the parties give their signature to confirm the existence of this fact and to affirm their wish that the legal matters arising in the case of the dissolution of the partnership entered into should be settled in accordance with the law.

W.W.: *Does the state not support marriages without content, which have nothing to do with the concept of marriage we discussed, like when people marry for certain financial incentives or marry foreigners pro forma in order to enable them to establish residency rights?*

W.Gädeke: Well, this is something which is related to the past because marriage and family are protected by the state. It is also perfectly legitimate for the state to want to ensure something of a healthy continuity, especially when you consider how much children suffer when marriage fails. In view of that it's perfectly understandable and also appropriate.

Such measures don't impose anything on the individual, he or she is free to arrange the contents of living together with a partner in complete autonomy. It is only certain consequences, such as rights and claims with regard to maintenance, old-age pensions, care of the children etc., which are not left up to the individual, because otherwise it would be a case of survival of the fittest. On the positive side marriage legislation aims at assuring proper fairness. How far this has been realized already is another matter. But as I have said already, the civil marriage legislation contributes nothing to the content of or the reasoning for the marriage.

Marriage as sacrament

W.W.: What is the purpose of marriage as a sacrament? Does the sacrament consist in the marriage ritual or is the marriage itself the sacrament?
W.Gädeke: There are different views on this. Marriage as a sacrament of Christendom is not all that old. It is the last of the seven sacraments and was not considered as such until the Middle Ages. Before that, the bridal couple only received a blessing in church. The original view is that the marriage is not concluded by the church wedding, through the sacrament, and not by the priest either, but that the marriage partners themselves conclude the marriage and make this known before the Godhead in order that the church, the religious community, may give it its blessing. This is the external understanding of marriage as sacrament. Originally marriage is viewed as something that is performed by the marriage partners living together.
W.W.: The concept of sacrament is hardly understood today. How can it be made accessible to a person who buys this book in a bookshop or a healthfood store and reads this interview with interest. How would you bring home to him or her what a sacrament is? What is the special extra ingredient added to a marriage through the sacrament, specifically the sacrament in the Christian Community? Can you express this in concrete terms?

W.Gädeke: Of course it is not possible for anyone to participate in the enacting of a sacrament if there is no familiarity
with sacraments. In the Christian Community it is really
only possible for people to become married who are
accustomed to co-perform sacraments in community religious life outside of marriage. What is special in the
Christian Community is that it is not simply performed by
the priest on his own, but it is the priest, the witnesses, the
bridal couple and the congregation who together perform
the sacrament. So it's not possible to just say: 'I will be
married in the Christian Community'.

To be be able to do this in the case of a marriage it is
necessary to have a certain amount of practice, of ability to
co-perform the sacraments. In the religious sacramental life
of the Christian Community there is no such thing as mere
recipients, but one is always a co-celebrant, as it were. For
the marriage ritual this means that one needs first to make
oneself capable, and that is brought about by a whole series
of conversations with the priest as well as active participation in the sacramental life of the community.

What is essential here is that the resolve to share one's life
together is afforded a religious quality through the
marriage ritual, a higher quality than in the case of such a
resolve before a registry office. The resolve to marry attains
a quality of a very definite wakefulness and consciousness;
this is expressed in the way the question is asked during the
marriage ritual. The question is not: Are you willing to take
this person in marriage?, but rather: Are you willing to raise
your resolve to live together with this other person to a level
where it is possible to say of this resolve that by it you walk
in the spiritual-divine world? The marriage preparation
talks are essentially focused on exploring what that
signifies.

*W.W.: Could you be more precise about what the concept of
sacrament actually means? Does the substance of a sacrament add
a special power or protection?*

W.Gädeke: In the concluding part of the marriage ritual there are also formulations which express a blessing. So this marriage is also blessed, not through the divine world alone, but also by virtue of the fact that the parners in marriage have brought the quality of their decision into their marriage. One could say that this blessing is partly a self-blessing. But that is no guarantee that a marriage concluded in this way will last for life.

W.W.: So we are really talking about the possible effect of a higher power?

W.Gädeke: Yes, but a power that doesn't emanate from the unique act of the marriage ritual alone; rather a power that requires continuous cultivation, that is, in the religious life which belongs to the manner in which a couple, married in this way, conduct their married life. In other words, the marriage ritual is not a one-time magic act but the beginning of the religious-sacramental life shared between the partners in marriage.

W.W.: What is the marriage witnesses' task in the Christian Community?

W.Gädeke: The witnesses to the marriage are not just witnesses in the sense that they bear witness to something seen or heard. This is important, too, and it is indeed their task in terms of the Christian Community to perceive the quality of the decision during the marriage ritual, to keep it alive in their consciousness and to continually re-enliven it in their memory. However, they are also witnesses in the sense that they contribute towards generating something, making something come into being. The witnesses to the marriage contribute towards making the marriage happen, by their inner religious deeds, by praying for the partners in marriage. This is an integral part of their decision to act as witnesses: the fact that they are willing to lend this assistance to the marriage partners' life together.

The Christian Community and anthroposophists

W.W.: Does one have to belong to the Christian Community in order to marry there?

W.Gädeke: The marriage is concluded somewhere else, as we have seen, but the marriage as a sacrament is an integral part of the religious life of the Christian Community. Even if a person is not yet a part of it in an outer sense, it is surely quite clear from what I have stated already that a person needs to be accustomed to participate in the sacraments in the form in which these live in the Christian Community. Whether the person concerned is outwardly, on paper, a member is of secondary importance. But the inner fact — being able to help carry out a sacrament — is an essential pre-requisite. It is perfectly alright to be at the very beginning of such a path, as far as the required *ability* is concerned, but there must be a genuine willingness to continue practising and cultivating this ability.

W.W.: Is the fact that someone is an anthroposophist in any way relevant to you as a priest; would you marry a person in the Christian Community on account of this person being an anthroposophist?

W. Gädeke: When someone is an anthroposophist this may have very positive effects because many of the matters relating to the sacrament, the religious life and the idea of marriage can be discussed more easily since an anthroposophist will have a particular understanding of certain of these concepts. But the marriage as a sacramental act is not dependent on someone being an anthroposophist. The preparation for it may be easier but is as esssential for an anthroposophist as it is for a non-anthroposophist.

W.W.: Are there concrete indications by Rudolf Steiner on the subject of marriage in relation to anthroposophists and The Christian Community?

W. Gädeke: The only sentence which is definitively known to have been said — with special reference to anthroposophists—is this: 'Of course, you must expect people who are married by you not just to remain totally uninvolved in all your other spheres. They must belong to you and help carry your work in the right way.' This statement remained unknown through decades, even in priest circles, and has only recently entered fully into the Christian Community priests' consciousness again. That is why things have not been done in accordance with that statement so far, or at least only in the rarest of cases. But in future it will certainly play an increasingly important part when it comes to such matters.

W.W.: Where is this sentence to be found?

W.Gädeke: This sentence comes from a conversation between Rudolf Steiner and the *'Oberlenkers'* [leaders] of the Christian Community on 18 January 1923.

Cultivation of marriage

W.W.: It might be appropriate, in view of the many marriage crises and divorces today, to say a few words about the ways in which a marriage can be cared for, whether it be enacted sacramentally in the Christian Community or otherwise.

W.Gädeke: What is needed to conduct and care for a marriage may be deduced from what we have already discussed. Of particular importance are the following efforts in the various areas concerned:

1. Continual work on inner questions, on the ways in which one views the world and the human being as such, on questions concerning religion and meaning. For the meaning of marriage can only be found and practised in the context of the overall question about the meaning of human existence.

2. Striving for shared soul experience, especially in art and in nature. A marriage will atrophy in the absence of a

consciously tended community of soul. This entails amongst other things continuously participating in the soul content of the other as well as allowing the other to participate in one's own.

3. Caring for (cultivating) the partnership of daily life. On the natural level this involves: as much temporal and spatial community as possible in the basic processes of life such as eating and sleeping. Learning to experience tenderness and sexuality to a higher degree as *life* processes as opposed to soul and body processes. And on a higher level: sharing a strong religious life together, as well as in a larger community. For this strengthens and transforms this area of the life forces.

4. Treating the physical partnership as little as possible as an end in itself but as a possibility to make real a communion of life, soul and spirit.

I am aware of the fact that this will sound very lofty and unattainable to many people. But I experience again and again that without such ideas and strivings married people get into hopeless situations of suffering, however well-intentioned they may be. I am convinced that without such ideas and strivings the fighting and the suffering in this area of life will become much exacerbated in the future.

3. Dealing With Problems – Before It's Too Late...

Wolfgang Weirauch: Looking at relationships – married or other partnerships involving two people – in connection with the fourth seven-year-period it is striking how many of these break up. These increasing break-ups are often initiated by the woman in the relationship, and frequently towards the end of her twenties. Which characteristics in the modern woman's constitution are responsible for this, and how can we understand this phenomenon?

Wolfgang Gädeke: We need to have a close look at the fourth seven-year-cycle in human life, in other words the age between 21 and 28, during which most long-term relationships are formed nowadays. In addition it is the best age for a woman to give birth. What are the special features of that phase of life? What should be accomplished in a person's biography during those seven years? What are the objectives of that fourth seven-year-span? From this we can develop the questions regarding the relationships which form in that time, as well as the concomitant crises and break-ups.

Natural crises at the end of the fourth seven-year-period

W.W.: Let's first focus on an incisive point in human development: how can we explain the crisis around the 26th/27th year from an anthroposophical point-of-view?

W.Gädeke: Rudolf Steiner gave two important indications with regard to this time at the end of the fourth seven-year-cycle. On the one hand he points out that the natural development of the human being through the various seven-year-periods — childhood, youth and early adult-hood — comes to an end around the 26th/27th year because the developmental forces are then used up. Any additional development, if at all, does not take place naturally but is initiated by the human being concerned if he wishes to bring it about through the forces of his 'I'. Rudolf Steiner also says that without working further on themselves, people nowadays don't progress beyond a natural age of 27 — even if they are 50.

W.W.: That is the so-called hypomochlion[5] is it not?

W.Gädeke: Yes, but that's not the same. The hypomochlion is around the 28th year; it is today very close to the point of crisis around the 26th/27th year and is something quite similar. If a human being is healthy and sound he will, in his 28th year, be in a state of balance between spirit and body, 'I' and matter, between spirit determination and body determination.

Body determination describes everything that comes to pass naturally. Of course it works beyond the 27th/28th year, but not as evolution but involution, which is expres-sed in coming closer to death, in the waning of the life forces, in the fact that growth ceases, etc.

Through the waning of bodily functions and life forces and the accumulating death forces there arises the possi-bility of enhanced powers of consciousness. However, the latter must be freely taken hold of by the 'I'. And the 28th year is a kind of still-point — the 'hypomochlion' — where these two possibilities — of the spirit and the body — should be in balance. But it also happens that the death-forces pre-dominate at a much earlier age, so that this hypomochlion is not around the 28th but, for example, around the 20th year; in prematurely-developed child geniuses it can be even earlier. Such people become senile very early on. But there are also people who live out of the forces of youth for a very long time, so that they really look like 25 when in actual fact they are 40.

W.W.: *A lot more could be said about the development or birth of the individual soul members; what happens specifically around the 28th year?*

W. Gädeke: It is the point in time which biographically marks the transition from the 'sentient soul' to the 'rational soul'. That means that the 'I', the actual individuality, can now take hold of itself in the fullest sense because it is no longer so strongly immersed in the sentient soul realm of feelings, needs and desires etc. — and can begin to free itself more effectively than was possible before. In the 28th year, when the death forces start to gain ascendency, the 'I'- consciousness assumes a greater power to illuminate the thinking consciousness; it is a feature of the rational soul period that the ability to think becomes more independent from the realm of feelings, from the sentient soul. In this way the 'I'-consciousness has the potential of attaining greater independence from body and soul; this potential is further enhanced in the 35th year when the 'consciousness soul' emerges.

W.W.: *Does this imply that a person who is still completely absorbed in the sentient soul is not able to accomplish any really free deeds — purely out of the spiritual — because he is as yet too strongly tied up with what goes on in his feelings?*

W.Gädeke: Well, the above applies to natural development. The development of civilization can, of course, put something of a spirit-orientated nature into a human being at an earlier stage, and in this way the sentient soul can well be illuminated by the spirit, as in the case of an ideal that a young person might carry. However, at this stage they are still totally related to the personal, to the soul. When an 18-year-old is enthusiastic about a teacher because that teacher inspires enthusiasm he may well absorb highly spiritual substance in that way. Even decisions can be made on such a basis, but these would not emanate from the young person's own spiritual self.

The success orientation of the male

W.W.: *How does a man experience himself in this fourth seven-year-period, and what is his core priority during that time?*
W.Gädeke: For centuries it has been taken for granted that the man finds his place in the world during that time. It is a fundamental priority in the male biography to do just that—whether in the form of an apprenticeship, study or any other vocational training. At the same time it is expected that the young man really gets to know the world during this period. Hence young men really did go out into the world in earlier days, they went off on their travels, whether to study or as travelling apprentices. The young man was expected to get away from his home and family, he had to put himself on his own feet and learn to cope with the new and different circumstances that came his way—a foreign people perhaps, or a totally new language.

When he then returned, towards the end of the fourth seven-year-period, he was able to settle down and embark on a socially more predictable existence in one place, because he had made his way in the world and knew that he could survive in it. Then he could also marry!

W.W.: *What about a man's soul experiences, what are his predominant orientations?*
W.Gädeke: A man's orientation in relation to the world entails that he wants and is expected to accomplish something that is accepted and needed by the world. This consciousness—to have to or want to accomplish something for the world—has a very high value in a man's soul. It is part of a man's natural make-up—maybe going back as far as ancient hunting culture, but most certainly throughout the last thousand years of our civilization, and it is, as such, not questioned by anyone. On the contrary—when a man shows a different orientation, for example, by exhibiting something of an escapist, drop-out mentality—this is certainly questioned.

W.W.: *How come that men are so strongly focused on what they accomplish — spiritually as well as in terms of concrete actions — and rather less so on other qualities or abilities of the soul?*

W.Gädeke: This is conditioned by the fact that a man is not able to draw his sense of self-worth from the physical body like a woman can since the male body is much harder, more earthly, more coarse and impermeable—hence more 'dead'—than a woman's. On average a man's lifespan is ten per cent shorter. The entire physical development of a man, from conception onwards, is characterized by a weaker life force. That means that a man, by virtue of his constitution, is not as strongly connected with nature and with the spiritual world as a woman. For the life forces, which in women are far stronger, are by their very nature something super-sensible, something spiritual—and that's why it is necessary for a man to compensate in the spiritual for his lack of life in his physical make-up; this he can do by accomplishing things which don't come to him naturally, but represent cultural achievements.

W.W.: *Is this the reason why he is more strongly affected than a woman when his accomplishment, i.e. that which he has to offer, is not wanted?*

W.Gädeke: Precisely. This is the reason why men cope less well with unemployment than women, although one must be careful not to create role stereotypes here ... like saying perhaps that it wouldn't do any harm if all women returned to the kitchen. Of course, women's unemployment needs to be tackled in the same way as men's; but from a psychological as well as from a constitutional standpoint a man finds it harder not to experience how his work and his actions are needed and accepted by the world around him. Such rejection can have a terribly paralyzing effect on a man, it can plunge him into despair, alcohol abuse etc.

W.W.: *Does a man rate his achievements, for example at work, higher than his relationship to a woman?*

W.Gädeke: In general, all personal human relationships take second place in the life of a man, that is in relation to the commitment and work he is willing to expend for the sake of it. The man lives in the consciousness and the expectation that the woman and the relationship ought to function, to work somehow. He then uses the relationship to refresh his own forces, as a zone of rest in his struggle for achievement outside. Therefore a man lacks the awareness that a relationship must be cultivated, which primarily involves work, commitment and time.

Instead he frequently holds the view that the relationship exists to give him strength, that he should be able to let himself go there and be taken by the woman as he is. It goes without saying that this applies, as everything said before, only to the average man. Exceptions do, of course, exist.

The human relationship as a woman's priority

W.W.: How would you characterize a woman's experience of a relationship, what is essential to her?
W.Gädeke: The human relationship is a woman's top priority! Hence her far greater willingness to opt out of training or career for the sole reason of taking better care of the relationship or saving it. If the man demands it, she will do almost anything because the human relationship is the most important thing of all to her and because she does not feel the urge to accomplish something for the world in the same way as a man. In a woman there arises more strongly instead the mothering drive accompanied by a sense of accomplishing something for the world by means of the children. And that is indeed the case!
W.W.: What is the constitutional reason for this in a woman?
W.Gädeke: Right from the outset a woman is permanently reminded by her entire bodily organism that she has all the pre-conditions for bearing children. At least every four

weeks she is made aware of this, again and again, and this takes place with an intensity that is completely beyond a man's experience. This alone indicates that woman is orientated – partially by instinct – to find fulfilment in the immediate human environment, to develop human relationships, including relationships to children which are, after all, human relationships too. So this is what is naturally there in a woman's soul and constitution, and not just as a result of upbringing and social conditioning.

And that's the problem: when this objective of the human relationship is the only one or if it strongly predominates, a partnership is not so easily possible.

Women in a partnership

W.W.: Can a woman who has a relationship with a man in her fourth seven-year-cycle actually ever attain her freedom and advance her ego development to the extent necessary today?
W.Gädeke: That depends very much on the nature of the relationship concerned. If a woman enters into a relationship before she has properly lived through the fourth seven-year-span or even starts a full partnership in her third seven-year span it will be extremely difficult for her to attain the degree of freedom which is, in fact, required. Because then the woman will be tied altogether to the man in the deeper layers of her being, particularly in the sphere of the life forces, and it is the very fact of being untied, of relying on one's own resources, of not depending on the other human being, which is so crucial to ego development in the fourth seven-year-span.
W.W.: So women therefore are less free within a partnership in this case?
W.Gädeke: That's right, and they don't claim this kind of freedom either. A man will carry on as he pleases, in his career, in his other work, even in terms of other relation-

ships. He claims his freedom and it doesn't occur to him to tie himself down in the way a woman does nor does he consider it necessary to be paying attention to what the woman might really want whilst he expects her to be attentive to what he wants.

The woman's ego development in human evolution

W.W.: With regard to the development of the ego a woman is generally in a very different position in life today than she was a few hundred years ago. What can be said about the woman's ego development from a human-biographical perspective?
W.Gädeke: Well, it is not just a matter of social oppression that women were not considered fully developed human beings in earlier times, not regarded as mature, and not even allowed as witnesses because it was held that their evidence could not be taken seriously. This wasn't just a case of patriarchal oppression, or chauvinism; it is simply a fact that the woman, in earlier times, was in truth not as individualized as the man on account of her living more strongly in the life and soul forces.

Indeed, the woman did not feel a need for individuation. This phenomenon may still be observed today to a certain extent: when young people want to go out and have fun you will often find that young men are quite prepared to do something on their own, whereas young women will mostly prefer to experience a concert in company with other people. A woman is inclined to want to experience whatever it may be together with the man she loves. This desire is not as prominent in a man, for if his wife does not wish to accompany him, it's not such a big deal for him, he just sets off alone.

This polarization between man and woman shows that the ego development of the man is more advanced. Rudolf Steiner says that the man lives more strongly in the polarity of ego and physical body, whereas the woman lives more strongly in the unity of soul and life forces. With regard to the development of the ego there is simply an over-emphasis in the man, and over the last hundred years a corresponding development has taken place for the woman as she also wants to be an ego, a person of completely equal rights.

W.W.: What in human evolution has caused this gradual breaking through of the woman's ego?

W.Gädeke: One important factor is certainly the intellectualization of the female soul as a result of education; furthermore the fact that women want to learn everything that our technical civilization demands. Even if a woman is not particularly inclined to technology and science our civilization has become such that she has to place herself within it. Just think what an important social event it was in earlier days when the women went to fetch water from the well — today they just turn on the tap; or what a great social occasion the village wash-day used to be when all the women laid out their linen on the grass to bleach, and so forth. Today a woman sticks her laundry into a machine, takes it out at some later time and hangs it up or sticks it into another machine. This leads to an impoverishment of social conditions and to an isolation of women.

W.W.: Is it appropriate to say that the ego-consciousness of the woman developed increasingly in the last 200 years in line with industrialization?

W.Gädeke: Yes, to the extent that women have integrated into the industrial work process; that certainly is part of the overall picture.

W.W.: Is it a general law in human development that the ego development of man and woman progresses rapidly but that the age-old gap is nevertheless maintained, with the man having developed his ego earlier and more strongly and therefore being more strongly tied to matter for ever after — or is the woman's ego development becoming more and more like that of the man?

W.Gädeke: This is not a straightforward issue inasmuch as the ego development attained by the man has its problematic aspects, too; it has contributed to bringing forth this technical culture whose deadening effects we are clearly confronted with today. The other side of the man's problematic ego development concerns the fact that he has lost his social instincts to a far greater extent than the woman. The advance of the man is by no means only positive.

It is of great importance that women discover the development of their own individuality, in other words a sense of self-determination, to be a worthwhile objective. Men can even help them in that, out of a new spirit of chivalry, provided that they understand that it is necessary for women today to undergo such an ego-development in a manner appropriate to their nature.

The individual ego-development of the man

W.W.: What does an ego-development entail for today's man? What experiences contribute to it?

W.Gädeke: One way might be for the young man to say to himself: 'I can survive in this world without father and mother, without a wife and without a steady human community around me.' This entails experiences which many young people seek even before their fourth seven-year-cycle, namely the experience of solitude. For example, I know a young man in one of the congregations who has gone to Alaska several times already in order to 'rough it' there and to challenge himself to survive by salmon-catching and so forth. Of course, in the final analysis this is illusory for one cannot in the long run survive in today's world on one's own without relapsing to the stage of hunter and gatherer. But the crucial thing is what is experienced in the soul as a result of living through a stage of total self-reliance.

This experience of solitude can be brought about by many different means. You don't have to go to Alaska for it, it is equally possible to have it in an inner-city tower block. The positive side of loneliness, of solitude, consists in learning to bear your own company; another way of doing this is, for example, to look at oneself in a mirror for quarter of an hour; this kind of confrontation with self is practically unbearable, but surely one prerequisite for growing up properly.

W.W.: But then a man in earlier times would not have experienced the kind of loneliness that almost every inhabitant in a big city finds himself in today. How did a man learn to bear this state of aloneness and self-reliance in recent centuries?

W.Gädeke: He learnt it through going journeying; travelling through the world on his own two feet cut him off from all his natural sources, from family, home, people and language. My father-in-law had this experience at the beginning of this century.

Such a thing as walking on your own two feet through the world was certainly tremendously conducive to developing a sense of being able to make it on your own.

The individual ego-development of the woman today

W.W.: How about the woman's ego-development in our time? Does she have to go through similar things to the man in earlier times, such as journeying?

W.Gädeke: I am personally convinced that this is also required of women today. Whilst I am not able to corroborate this with any indication by Rudolf Steiner, my experience tells me that comparable experiences are necessary for a woman.

W.W.: Could you explain this in some more detail?

W.Gädeke: Part of it would be that young women do not let their parents make all the arrangements for them, and that they enter into actions to which they don't feel naturally inclined — such as setting up their own bank account, dealing with the authorities themselves, going through the usual hassles with civil servants and superiors without outside help, getting to grips with the legal aspects of life, and so forth. It is of decisive importance that they are not relieved of these kind of involvements, and I also think that it is very beneficial for a girl to encounter totally different situations.

My niece, for example, went to South Africa for a year, and this had a very positive effect on her growing up. It can be an important experience to fall sick in a place far away from home. with no parents or close friends to support you, and to find out that one can survive nevertheless. Bearing such a thing gives you maturity!

Of course, this 'journeying' of the young woman today doesn't have to follow the patterns of the young journeymen of earlier days, but the experiences of self-reliance, of solitude, of making your way in the world are crucial for women today. In my view this also entails that a woman determines as one of her aims in life a proper training and education, and a real accomplishment in the world, an accomplishment for the benefit of other people. It is even better if the woman completes her education or training and works for a number of years in her chosen profession in order to get to know all the difficulties — working with colleagues, hierarchical structures, money, extortion, ambition etc. — which are encountered in these environments; in this way she will have experienced for once the miserable aspects which form part of a man's everyday life.

When a woman breaks out of an unfree relationship

W.W.: In summary: a woman who has no experience of working life, of being self-reliant, of having coped with solitude, is unlikely to have developed her ego sufficiently to survive in a relationship with a man, and the relationship is likely to break up as she approaches the age of thirty.

W. Gädeke: Yes, I think so, for a relationship for life, a life partnership implies that one jointly dwells in the same location — the exact opposite of what I just described. Hence, in the olden days, a man was often only allowed to marry at 28, when he had all that behind him and was settled with a trade or career. The desire for freedom, the longing for a state of not being tied down, for spontaneousness, for committing follies is something totally natural, provided that these follies don't have catastrophical social effects. Such spontaneous and maybe foolish actions should ideally only have repercussions on oneself, but as soon as you live in partnership there will be other people who are affected, especially when there are children.

Therefore it is invariably far better for a woman to have gone through all these kinds of experiences before she ties herself to a man; then she will feel: 'I could survive without him! If the relationship breaks up it won't be the end of me. I know that I can survive without my husband!'

W.W.: *Assuming that a woman in her fourth seven-year cycle has not gone through such solitary experiences and has therefore missed out on the concomitant individuation — I would think this applies to many women — and assuming that she has been living in a steady relationship for a number of years, what is the likely outcome?*

W.Gädeke: The woman will strongly adapt to the man, she will makes his aims her own, maybe even make him the prop of her self-confidence or attach herself to him so strongly that she believes in the end that she is lost without him. This sense of being nothing without him, however, is something which will not carry her beyond the 28th–30th year, for then she will herself rebel against it. This state of being unfree and tied-down will eventually prove intolerable.

W.W.: The 28th year is the decisive point in this case as well then?
W. Gädeke: In my experience this point is reached somewhere between 25 and 33. At some time in that period
women experience an intense desire for freedom, maybe
leave husband and children in the lurch, start or feel the
need to quickly do some training and so forth. It happens
around the thirtieth year that a woman tries to catch up
with all the things she has not done yet, and as a rule this
results in chaos, especially when there are children.

The etheric sheath: basis of married life

*W.W.: It may not have become suffiently clear yet to the reader
why relationships are practically bound to founder when the
female partner's ego-development is insufficient. On the one hand
we have the striving for freedom and the strengthening of the sense
of 'I' in the woman around the end of her twenties, and on the other
something that works against freedom: the shared etheric sheath
with the life partner. What is that etheric sheath, how is it formed?*
W.Gädeke: This is indeed the most difficult thing in the
marriage as this whole realm of human life is furthest
removed from our consciousness. We are conscious of the
many important parts of our physical bodies. But that in-
between layer, our habit, our temperament, our memory
sphere—this realm of the etheric body is largely removed
from our waking consciousness. That's why it is so difficult
to really be aware of what actually happens in a relationship.

Indeed, in sharing a life together, the life force of woman
and man merge. From the outside it looks as if there were
still two separate people, but when people live in partnership there is such a thing as a joint biography which
develops, there are shared memories, common habits are
formed, common rhythms of sharing meals and sleeping
together. This all belongs in the realm of the life forces, and

these shared things create a tremendously strong connection. One becomes merged with the other, as it were, in this part of one's being; the longer the relationship endures the more intense this will be. Then it's no longer possible to conquer the world and get to know it in the way that a single person is still able to in the fourth seven-year-period, neither is it possible to experience solitude because one is merged with the other.

Therefore, any soul-spiritual striving for self-autonomy, the desire to decide for oneself, to do things under one's own steam, to look at the world from one's own point of view instead of always together with one's partner or through his eyes – works against this community of life forces, and leads to terrible tension, to crucial tests. Either ego-development is then abandoned and the woman submits to the constraints of the relationship whilst renouncing her own liberation, or the etheric sheath, the life partnership, is damaged.

W.W.: How could one explain to a layman the kind of forces that make up this etheric sheath? How is it formed? By eating together, sleeping together, having sexual relations? Are there priorities?

W. Gädeke: One should think of it as the effects of supersensible forces; primarily these are life forces. We clearly experience the effects of these forces, for example, in feeling tired or wide awake, well or ill. These life forces can be experienced particularly strongly, and also encouraged, wherever there is rhythm in life, rhythmic repetition. For life is repetition in rhythmical processes. Be it the rhythms of the internal organs, the rhythms of day and night or the rhythms of a woman's monthly cycle – all life processes are dependent on rhythms.

A community of life rhythms starts to evolve as soon as people begin to live together rhythmically, in seeing each other every day, in having daily meals together, in sleeping together in the same room – I mean real sleeping – in passing from waking to sleeping together, and so forth. The life forces which each possesses individually start to harmonize to the same rhythm, at the same intervals, in unison with another person.

Think of how much it means to older married couples to have shared memories over decades! How significant it is that they are so attuned to one another in their mutual behaviour that entire habits are interwoven, complementing one another! All of this indicates that the etheric forces are strongly knitted together.

W.W.: *Would this explain the similarities in physiognomy one often finds in older couples?*

W. Gädeke: Yes, this is also an effect of the community of life forces.

W.W.: *You referred to etheric forces moving in the partners' etheric bodies to the same rhythm. How does this relate to the shared etheric sheath – is the sheath an additional conglomerate of forces or energies, a special spiritual-spatial body?*

W. Gädeke: It should be envisaged as something spiritual-spatial: a kind of space that is created. It may be a funny comparison, but imagine birds, swallows, for example, lined up on a telegraph line at definite distances from each other. If two of these birds are actually *married*, they sit very close to each other, in body contact as it were, billing and cooing. There you have the outer expression of something common which envelops them both. It's not just between them at a distance, but this *between* becomes so strong that it envelops them both. One could imagine it as two spheres approaching one another and eventually interpenetrating.

W.W.: *Is this etheric sheath only effective when there is a physical-spatial closeness or also at a distance? Does it tear after a while when people have separated?*

W.Gädeke: I wouldn't call it tearing, but it does gradually disintegrate for the etheric forces are tied to the physical, spatial body as long as we are living in the body. Hence it's entirely appropriate for the law to define marriage as 'a long-term relationship running a shared household'. The etheric sheath depends on people living together in a shared space. But it is possible to maintain a soul-spiritual relationship at a distance, as that is independent of space.

Other etheric communities

W.W.: Are etheric sheaths also formed between other people, such as between parents and children, siblings or other types of communities?

W.Gädeke: Certainly! There are many etheric communities of this kind, and the whole family with children is certainly a case in point, especially when the children are still small. But etheric sheaths also begin to form between people who work together as colleagues, in particular when they have a lot to do with each other, developing strong common habits and rhythms. But in such cases the sheath is not that strong because they generally don't eat or sleep together.

W.W.: Does such an etheric sheath begin to develop between friends who do not yet entertain a community of bed and table?

W.Gädeke: Yes, but very tentatively so – insofar as they meet repeatedly. In most cases there is a certain repetitive element, and anything connected with the life forces should always be viewed in context with a long duration of time. It's not a matter of hours but of months and years; so it is perfectly possible for an etheric sheath to be formed around people whose relationship would not normally be considered a marriage.

Necessity and freedom in a community of life forces

W.W.: Why is it that such an etheric sheath leads to the impairing of the free nature of a relationship in a way that the woman in the partnership experiences as oppressive?

W.Gädeke: When a person's individuality has fully developed, i.e. when the person has gone through experiences of aloneness and of 'standing on their own feet', then he or she can freely decide to commit himself or herself to a community of life forces. But when these experiences have not been lived through fully, the 'I' will always retain a longing to catch up and live this out. But it cannot really do so when the person concerned—in the deeper layers of his or her nature—is so strongly tied.

The 'I' does not require this state of freedom throughout a whole lifetime, but it must have had the following experience: 'This commitment, this togetherness [literally *life community*] this growing together into one etheric sheath is something I have freely chosen. And even if this etheric sheath breaks, as a result of death or divorce, I shall be able to carry on with my life, I will still be whole.' If a relationship has been entered upon in any kind of dependence, this experience will be missing.

W.W.: *But the etheric sheath strongly determines the sense of autonomy of partners in a relationship who haven't developed their individuality sufficiently by the end of the fourth seven-year-cycle, is that right?*

W.Gädeke: Precisely. But when the 'I', the individuality, has been developed prior to entering into a relationship, the commitment to a partner can be freely willed. Then the 'I' will not be irritated by a sense of being tied down, because it has experienced that freedom. That's why it is so important to have made one's own choices and to have experienced real freedom in the fourth seven-year-cycle.

Furthermore it is necessary for the 'I' to understand the meaning of marriage so that this community of ether forces is not just experienced as constraint and imprisonment but rather as something which the 'I' has wished for once and continues to want—with an aim in mind. When I really want something because I know *why* I want it I will not be constrained by it! In other words, this commitment, this etheric sheath, only appears unfree because one doesn't understand it and is not conscious of why one wants it.

In short, the question can only be answered if at the same time one understands the purpose of the relationship and makes it one's personal ideal and wants it for that very reason. Then the 'I' need not feel unfree in the slightest.

Relationships in the fourth seven-year-period: between self-determination and a sense of security

W.W.: Let's take a possible scenario in your marital counselling: a man and woman, both twenty-something, meet in the underground, fall in love and want to stay together. What do you advise them?

W.Gädeke: I would encourage them to cultivate their relationship by all means, especially to work on building up a community in soul and spirit, and at the same time exercise as much restraint as possible, proceed very carefully with anything reaching into the etheric — anything representing physical repetition. Of course it's not fashionable today to say things like this, but it is a fact: as soon as sexual union becomes a regular feature, a matter of fact, a community of life forces inevitably arises. Then it's quite immaterial how often people tell themselves that they're not married and the like, because *de facto* one is married as soon as such a community of life forces is established.

In the past this time of restraint was imposed from outside — at first there was the engagement, and during that time you dealt with each other at a distance; and today one might actually strive for this out of insight, on the basis of understanding why one's doing it, namely to enable both partners to seek and live through the experiences of aloneness and of freedom we characterized before. It really is possible.

W.W.: What form would this period between getting to know one another and forming a settled relationship take? Would you, for

*example, advise these young people not to move in with each
other?*

W.Gädeke: Yes, absolutely! If the young people concerned
were at all willing to hear it I would invariably say: 'Don't
set up home together, because if you do you are effectively
marrying, but you have basically not reached the stage yet
when you can truly marry! Try and keep your relationship
on a level — in the physical sense, too — that you don't enter
into this absolute commitment. First of all try to help each
other to go through these experiences of being free, of not
being tied, in spite of your friendship.'

Sometimes it is helpful not to be living in the same town,
and not to keep in touch by telephone but write letters
instead, in order to raise the relationship to an objective
level; one might, for example, exchange views about what
marriage actually is: 'Do we want to marry? Why? What are
our longings, really? What is our aim? What is merely
wishful?'

Well, there is a great deal one could write to one another
about. It's also a wonderful thing to travel together and to
experience some of the richness of the world, different
landscapes, different aspects of civilization, with the other
person. There are so many ways of furthering a friendship
which don't involve setting up home together. But generally, young people of that age are totally set on living
together. In that case the crisis-like developments towards
the end of the twenties are bound to occur. In the absence of
a deeper understanding of what that age demands there
will, inevitably, be these tremendous ruptures in the
relationship, with totally incompatible longings breaking
through: the striving for freedom and autonomy on the one
hand and the striving for closeness, familiarity and warmth
on the other. These struggles can take on phenomenal
proportions, both within a person and between the
partners.

W.W.: *Might your recommendations not be taken as a new* *prudishness — in other words, relationships without sex? Is that what's intended?*

W.Gädeke: Well, there are different ways of looking at it for it hasn't got much to do with prudishness. I am not saying that there must be no sex! But I am saying — in line with the way in which Rudolf Steiner formulates the order of social life — the more people succeed in initially keeping sexuality out of such youthful friendships, the better they manage to keep the physical aspect of their relationship on a level of tender affection, the freer and easier and more harmonious the individual's ego development and hence the development of the relationship will be. The degree to which an individual manages to do without sexual activity is his individual problem or destiny. In any case, I am not saying that it has to be so — I am saying that if they don't manage to do without and insist on living together there will be the consequences I have described. It has nothing to do with prudishness or moralizing, it's simply a question of pointing out the consequences ...

W.W.: *... because of the etheric sheath forming?*

W.Gädeke: Yes, for that merging inevitably takes place.

W.W.: *But what about travelling together, which you recommend ... doesn't this also further the development of such etheric forces between the partners?*

W.Gädeke: Of course, because in such a case you intermittently live together from morning until evening. It's perfectly good to try this every now and again, why not? It is important to experience the other partner in different everyday situations — unlike engagements in the past, where this was confined to a stiff sofa at the weekends. In this light it's a good idea to go away travelling together, but it doesn't follow that one has to live together permanently.

When the woman goes out into the world...

W.W.: *Is the most important point we have established now in relation to the young couple, that you would advise the woman to go out into the world, say for a year, before setting up home with a man?*

W.Gädeke: Yes, something along those lines, but I would not spell out the length of time. It may well be that the decisive experiences have been met in a year, but it's equally possible that they haven't even in two years. It is very individual. It's important to determine what measure of freedom has been attained in the period concerned, to what extent the longing to meet the world, to go out into the world, to be free and untied, has really been satisfied.

I would like to mention something from my own experience: As a young man and student I was a passionate dancer, and suddenly, at age 25, it was all over. I had a distinct feeling that I no longer needed to dance through the nights in glamourous ballrooms. It wasn't that somebody had dissuaded me nor was it a case of asceticism, it was simply over. In addition, I felt a new sense of calm, there was no longer a feeling of possibly missing out on things. Maybe there is a certain measure of being 'footloose and fancy free' that one just has to have tasted to the full. Others might feel this in relation to travelling; then they will do it until it is no longer felt as a strong need. But I would never look at it from a sort of kill-joy perspective, a forced asceticism, that would not work.

W.W.: *Let's turn our attention to our young couple again: Let's assume the woman takes the decisive and right step, at the right time, and goes away somewhere in order to develop her individuality. Isn't the most likely outcome – as the woman is only just learning to stand on her own feet and is at the same time, by force of her constitution, always striving towards a relationship – that she will leave her partner behind and then, because she can't endure being on her own, look for a new one at the new place she is at?*

W.Gädeke: That would just signify that this relationship was not deep and mature enough, and then it's also fine if it breaks up. In that case it was a relationship which had all the right ingredients to turn into a friendship, but not a partnership, a relationship for life. It must also be considered that at all events one is far too strongly connected with those people one meets during one's youth. Very often the inner freedom that is needed for entering into a proper relationship can simply not be there. From the point of view of destiny there may be real knots. You can observe this in many friendships between young people, for example in the case of real love-hate relationships when the partners cannot leave one another, but cannot coexist either.

W.W.: These love-hate relationships and other problematic friendships between young people, what sort of relationships are they from a deeper perspective?

W.Gädeke: It is necessary to consider the idea of reincarnation in this context. The more intense and problematic a relationship was in previous incarnations the more intense the destiny in this life. A great closeness in destiny does not augur well for a marriage or similar relationship. To be able to opt for a commitment to another person out of insight and free will, there should basically be a very high degree of freedom with regard to karmic involvement. If, however, the relationship is already largely determined by destiny, karmically tight and consolidated, the possibilities of working it out freely are limited.

Rudolf Steiner once said in a conversation during the Munich rehearsals for the Mystery Dramas – with reference to a personality in the Mystery Dramas – that nowadays it is not only undesirable to marry a blood relative, but also siblings or relatives from previous lives. I take this to indicate that karmic closeness rather speaks against a union for life. One can occasionally observe in relationships between young people how very much alike the two people forming a couple are, even in physiognomy, although they are not related. There is a youthful picture of Assja Tur-genieff and her husband A. Belyi where this is extremely striking. So I would always advise caution in these youthful friendships since there is often old destiny involved which might hinder the successful forming of a partnership for life.

The need to establish one's ego versus the desire for loving care

W.W.: Given that a choice must be made, is it more important for a woman in her third or fourth seven-year-cycle to live through her ego-experiences than to maintain a relationship?

W.Gädeke: The former is rather more important than rescuing a particular relationship at all costs. Of course, some women find this exceedingly difficult. But if they really search for the answer in their innermost being they might be able to say: 'Yes, I really do want this!' In many cases it is only their soul's striving towards a relationship or the continuing of a relationship which opposes this.

W.W.: Are the two things incompatible for the woman of today – a relationship to bring comfort in all situations of suffering on the one hand, and the finding of her own individuality by means of experiences of aloneness on the other?

W.Gädeke: I am convinced that this is no longer possible side-by-side for women today. Of course, the same applies to men, there is no great difference. It's only that a man can claim for himself that kind of freedom and aloneness within a relationship whereas a woman can never do that.

Practical advice for youth friendships

W.W.: To help safeguard a youthful friendship from breaking apart while the woman goes out into the world, what practical advice do you give for this transitional period?

W.Gädeke: Writing letters to each other, as mentioned before, is definitely a good thing as it helps raise the relationship onto a more objective and higher spiritual level, which is not possible in a quick telephone conversation. To write a letter one has to learn to express oneself clearly and in addition one is able to respond to the other in a measured way—in contrast to reacting out of the moment. This makes it possible to cultivate the relationship properly.

Of great importance for this bridging period is cultivating the soul-relationship. How do I let the other participate in my experiences through my letters? This is an essential point. This exchange, this mutual participation in the other's soul content is of great importance in a marriage, too.

A correspondence also offers the opportunity to deal with the important spiritual questions: 'What is the meaning of life for you, for me? Do we have a shared sense of meaning? What is the nature of ideals? Which ideals will we strive after together?'

W.W.: What else is important for such a period of bridging a prolonged absence?

W.Gädeke: If it is possible to conduct an exchange of views on spiritual questions by writing letters to each other, it's also a good idea to delve into religious questions and ask oneself, for example, whether one is willing to pray for one another or make a connection via a particular verse or meditation. There really are manifold ways of cultivating a relationship through an exchange on the level of soul and spirit.

This does not imply that one should never meet in person, but by way of dealing with one another on a soul-spiritual level the focus of the relationship is shifted into that realm where we are most likely to be free.

W.W.: Let's consider once again the couple who fell in love on the underground: in their state of being-in-love they will care precious little for all these things — not to live together, establishing their individuality through aloneness etc. What would have to happen so that these matters, which are of existential importance for a relationship, are really considered?

W.Gädeke: I have been trying for twelve years now to offer courses in marriage for young people, and I have conducted quite a few and look forward with anticipation to what effect, if one may put it like this, they have had. In addition, I have discussed such matters with quite a number of young people on an individual basis. To what extent the people concerned find the strength to carry out what has been discussed is another question altogether.

But even if they don't manage they nevertheless know that this is what they wanted and that they must attribute the consequences to themselves. They can no longer blame their ignorant parents or society at large for their misery.

W.W: *You are basically saying the knowledge of all things connected with marriage needs to somehow flow into the general consciousness in our culture so that young people get a greater awareness of these things before they contemplate a partnership?*

W.Gädeke: Yes, that would be desirable. I also discuss matters of this kind in upper school religion lessons. A kind of study of biography and community, a study of the community of the sexes ... because these things simply have to be taught and learnt! And there are certain aspects and inner laws with which everyone should be acquainted. What he subsequently does with that knowledge is the individual's own affair — he is of age and free — and society today must no longer enforce these things from outside because then they cannot live as ideals.

There are many young people today who really have an acute awakeness vis-à-vis the problems of marriage, and who are aware of relationships falling to pieces all around them, but very often they have no idea why! Insofar as people are definitely highly sensitized with regard to this problem, there is a real opportunity to try and achieve something for the future by proper conscious learning and genuine consultation.

Relationships between younger women and older men

W.W.: Let us look at another hypothetical case of a relationship. A girl, not quite twenty years old, her father died prematurely, hence she has an intense longing for a man ... a man twice her age steps on the scene. Would it be too harsh to say that such a marriage is bound to result in servitude on the part of the woman as she will not be able to develop her individuality in the context of such a union, or else that the marriage will break when the woman approaches the end of her twenties?

W.Gädeke: I have never come across a case of such a marriage or partnership surviving in the long term. I am not claiming that such marriages do not exist, but I haven't come across a case, where a girl of 17 or 18 enters into a relationship with a man of say ten years older who has largely completed his ego-development in the masculine manner and the girl becomes his concubine, as it were, and where that marriage did not founder. In my experience—I am thinking of specific destinies now—such marriages break up even earlier, that is, when the woman is in her middle twenties. Whilst not wishing to generalize I still have to say that this is my experience.

Three possibilities in the course of a marriage

W.W.: We may draw the following conclusions from what we have discussed so far which apply to our time today and to Central European culture in general: in principle there are only three possibilities for a life partnership (and a fourth which we haven't addressed yet):

a) the woman has sufficiently developed her individuality and likewise the man; hence the prospects for a fulfilling marriage for life are good.

b) The woman enters into the partnership at too young an age and

has not developed her individuality as is needed; the marriage survives but only because the woman subordinates herself.
c) The marriage breaks up.
W.Gädeke: That's a fair way of putting it!
W.W.: *Even in the face of rapidly growing divorce rates and a declining number of marriages entered into, there surely are still a number of intact marriages which are not hollow and empty and into which the woman has entered at a young age without having developed her individuality. Would one say in the case of such couples that their relationship is bound to be a scenario of domineering man and submissive woman?*

W.Gädeke: I would never put it so generally even if it can be backed statistically — individually it might still be inaccurate. For there is always a possibility of catching up with certain developmental steps even within a marriage. It is possible to acquire certain abilities later on, but then only with great effort and difficulties.

Let's assume a couple got married at age 22. Now they are both 30, the woman feels an intense urge for freedom, maybe the man, too, if he hasn't developed his ego properly yet; I am not insisting that it is totally impossible to catch up with things even after ten years of marriage, but generally there needs to be a great deal of skilled support to make it happen because most people are not at all aware of why things don't work out.

At the grave of civilization

W.W.: *That implies that a very stark conclusion must be drawn from human relationships today: there will be no way forward in the realm of marriage unless all the aspects pertaining to marriage are clearly understood. Rudolf Steiner once said that unless civilization as a whole is enlivened by anthroposophy by the end of the century we will be standing at the grave of all civilization;[6] can one relate this also to the problems of marriage?*

W.Gädeke: I am convinced that in the long run men and women will not be able to share their lives in a way appropriate to the human being unless proper spiritual cognition is applied to this issue. But we are talking averages here, there are always individual cases where the marriage works, for example when people still live out of old forces, etc.

I know a couple who have been married for eighteen years. They did not encounter anthroposophy until much later but they survived an awful lot of trials because they were still so healthy within themselves and had both brought a great deal of social forces into the marriage. There are individual cases like this!

But just look around you, where do you find that still? At best people stay together because of social pressures, or, as in the case of a couple of farmers, because the farm would go to rack and ruin. There may be other economic pressures, or even no other option for the woman. That is really very common! But these kind of pressures will apply less and less in future.

W.W.: What is the nature of the forces of which older couples may still avail themselves today, and why are they on the decline?

W. Gädeke: Part of these forces are the social instincts, for example that which connects people by virtue of belonging to the same nation, or having grown up in the same environment and speaking the same dialect. Such things make for strong connections! These forces all derive from natural forms of community and are ultimately the effects of those spiritual beings Rudolf Steiner calls the 'group souls' and which have worked through the blood ties between people and connected them in soul. These group souls are working less strongly now, they are withdrawing. This is the deeper reason for people's growing sense of isolation and their asocial nature. But it is a necessary development, a pre-condition for the evolvement of the consciousness soul, the enhanced potential of the human 'I' to address itself to what is purely spiritual.

The fourth possibility: finding one's 'I' within the marriage

W.W.: Could we look in depth now at one other aspect, namely the possibility of conducting a partnership, the possibility of establishing one's individuality, finding one's 'I' in the context of marriage! You already hinted at that fourth possibility which involves catching up with the process of finding one's individuality, one's 'I' on the part of the woman, maybe also of the man, within an existing marriage, without gradually devaluing or even breaking the relationship. You said that such a thing is possible, albeit very difficult. How would the two partners go about this?

W.Gädeke: It can be done but it does require the conscious approach to marriage I have already outlined, or else it won't succeed. Much depends on what the marriage has been like so far, and in particular on the number of children already in the family.

Let's take a case I know of at present where the woman had already got three children by the age of 21, but then no more. These young people are open to receiving a great deal of counselling because they realize that they had a difficult start. Now they are in their mid-twenties, she wants to undergo some training and he is the stay-at-home husband, as it were.

W.W.: A softie?

W.Gädeke: No, he's not a softie, not by any means, he's a typically masculine type of man—intellectual and strong-willed. If they both agree that intensive marital counselling is essential they stand a good chance.

W.W.: But what is it that a woman has to do to find her individuality in the context of marriage? Does she have to leave, or start a training or what...?

W.Gädeke: She cannot completely catch up with what was omitted. The kind of freedom one is able to enjoy in one's fourth seven-year-cycle, unencumbered by husband and children, can never be fully reproduced, no matter how much love and consideration is given by the other, no matter how much freedom one manages to claim for oneself. But *something* can be achieved in this direction: the woman can undertake some training, she might meet other people in the process and form new relationships and friendships. Of course this entails strain on the marriage for it will have an effect on the time that can be spent with the other partner.

W.W.: *Let's assume a case now where the children are still of an age that the woman is obliged to take care of them herself. Isn't there something specific you could recommend, some practical advice how the woman in such a relationship might still develop her individuality? For example, would it be appropriate for her to aim for some kind of intellectual achievement in order to drive forward her ego-development within the limits of a short period every day which she might allot to this purpose, as far as her commitments with children and marriage allow? I am thinking of an involvement that is totally hers, for which she alone is responsible, without any kind of help from her husband.*

W.Gädeke: Yes, that would be a possibility; if she is able to pursue some form of study from home, be it something like the Open University or any other form of engaging with things that requires mental activity—such as anthroposophy or religion, or whatever. If it is done out of her own resolve, if she does it because she wants to do it, for herself and not for her husband because he expects it of her or is himself engaged with whatever it may be, if she really accomplishes it out of her innermost impulses it may very well serve the development of her individuality.

However, if her children are still in the first seven-year-cycle, their etheric bodies, on account of not having been freed yet, will still be tightly interwoven with their mother's. That makes it extremely difficult for a woman to muster the forces of consciousness required for mental/ spiritual endeavours; the life forces are not always sufficient to sustain it. Some women even express this by saying that during the time of pregnancy or breast-feeding they feel in a sort of bovine state. During that time there is an extremely strong call on the life forces and that necessarily restricts the forces of consciousness. In extreme cases it can even go so far that women say to themselves: 'I am not even here!' They experience themselves as 'pushed aside'.

W.W.: *So the culmination of demands on the woman during pregnancy and breast-feeding is virtually bound to result in marital crises?*

W.Gädeke: Absolutely! Any experience of the 'I', the development of the ego, the liberation of the ego — it's always connected to processes of consciousness, and these are death processes. I am not saying that pregnant women or women with small children are not capable of mobilizing these conscious forces, but it is very difficult.

W.W.: *Would you nevertheless advise a woman — if it is her ego-development that is of paramount importance — to try and arrange for short periods, maybe an hour every day, even during pregnancy, breast-feeding and caring for very small children, in which she may devote herself to conscious activity, inspite of the death processes involved?*

W.Gädeke: Well, the question would arise whether it absolutely has to be mathematics, or whether it might not be better to read fairy-tales, or study the myths of different peoples or anything else more related to the life forces as opposed to the forces of consciousness.

W.W.: *But this wouldn't be enough to encourage the sense of achievement which is vital to the development of the ego. I'm thinking of a shaky marriage situation where the woman, on account of being a mother, breastfeeding etc., experiences a growing sense of unfreedom, almost imprisonment and is hoping* *that some form of intellectual achievement might be the answer to keep her sane in the marriage.*

W.Gädeke: That would imply a real risk for the children, on account of the inherent nature of processes of consciousness, of dealing with dead matters. Such involvement is likely to take something away from the children. Children react to that with nervousness and insecurity, the mother becomes impatient etc. For the children's sake the woman needs this vegetative brooding while they are below seven. I am far from implying something negative here. The woman should be able to bear it because she knows: 'I have had the other type of experience, and I will regain it some time. Now it's not on the agenda.'

Non-domineering men

W.W.: *So far we have pictured a typically average man — intellectual and strong-willed — in relation to whom a woman feels restricted in her freedom. How is it in relationships where the man's make-up is not quite so typically masculine, not so domineering and where the woman, as a result, does not become so acutely aware of the limitations to her freedom?*

W.Gädeke: Of course it is easier in a certain sense when the characteristics relating to gender are not so extreme, when a man is able to appreciate the female virtues as proper abilities, maybe even finds enjoyment in taking on certain of the roles traditionally attributed to women—but the basic problem remains the same! There are factors in such a man's constitution and inclination of soul which make things easier, but it will never do away with the problem, for a man—however soft and gentle—can never reach the same state as the woman.

Preparation for marriage: a summary

W.W.: As far as preparation for marriage is concerned the requirements might be summarized as follows: an exact and comprehensive knowledge of the different way in which men and women are constituted in soul, spirit and body; establishing the meaning of marriage to both partners, the need for both to have established their individuality by experiencing solitude and by means of confronting unfamiliar social conditions, introduction to all these problem areas in the third seven-year-cycle, if possible. Anything missing?

W.Gädeke: Nothing essential.

Marital counselling: marital problems are not individual

W.W.: You have been working as a marriage counsellor for many years now. Could you describe some of the basic features of this kind of counselling? How do you go about it? What kind of people approach you?

W. Gädeke: I consider it a rare case of luck if the man comes along right from the start, because in most cases the woman will first come by herself. When it does happen I tend to praise the man for doing it because it's a fact that men need praise for their accomplishments, especially when they do something which is not in their nature, something they had to struggle with. Besides there is in such cases a very genuine reason for praising the man involved, as men find it very much more difficult than women to accept help in the first place. In other words, a certain mood has to be created at the beginning of the counselling process.

Then things will also depend a bit on whether I know the people concerned or not. If I don't know them at all I will say a few general things at first, for example, that I am familiar with their marital problems before they set about telling me about them. If necessary—for example when the people concerned are inhibited—I offer to summarize their problems in my own words.

W.W.: How do people react when you tell them that you know their problems already?

W. Gädeke: I have experienced that sort of situation with women whom I did not know and who did not know me and who had been referred by their doctors. I told them that the problems were always the same, in their case, too. Naturally, people find it difficult to conceive of this for they experience their problems in a very individual way. Women tend to react with incredulity and astonishment because they cannot understand how their own problems could possibly be general problems.

In such situations, which are not always easy, the woman concerned tends to ask me to explain what I mean. I will then describe the five or six marriage problems to which everything can be reduced. On the last occasion I did this, the woman looked at me in amazement and said: 'Everything you described applies to me'. When people can establish that one is familiar with their problems before they have voiced them, a certain mood of trust is created.

It is different when he—although it is mostly she—wishes to talk on their own account. I will of course encourage them to do so whilst making absolutely clear that problems in the marriage are completely natural today and that everyone who is married will encounter them. It is normal that 98 per cent of people today suffer from tooth decay, and having problems in your marriage is as normal as that. Once people find out that it is not just their partner or they themselves that are inadequate enough to be in that situation, or when they find out that it is simply not true that they are alone in suffering such a difficult destiny or being tied up with such a dreadful partner, they experience a kind of liberation.

Overcoming the inability to communicate with one's partner — two examples

W.W.: Let's look at a specific case: A couple sits in front of you, they have been married for quite some time, their children have left home, their communication has broken down more and more, they are fed-up with each other and are contemplating a separation.

W.Gädeke: When the communication between two people has broken down, it is important to establish whether they are in any way concerned with questions about the meaning of marriage, whether they are religious or not, whether there is an openness to anthroposophy, and so forth. All of this will have an effect on the starting point.

For example, I counselled a couple once in which the woman was a member of the Christian Community whereas the man wasn't, although he was close to the Christian Community. They had come to this kind of lack of communication; their children had left home. In their case two counselling sessions were sufficient; we exchanged views on how talking together can be encouraged. These two then read a piece of text together and re-discovered by way of talking to each other about this objective text how one can talk to each other about subjective soul contents.

W.W.: So you set them the reading of these texts as homework?

W.Gädeke: Yes, I did. Of course we talked before about what sort of text might be suitable, and I tried to give some guidance on what direction it might take. After two consultations their inability to converse had been overcome; however, this was very unusual, in most cases it's not as easy as this.

W.W.: Can one say that in most cases an understanding of the meaning of marriage is lacking?

W.Gädeke: Yes, it's absolutely essential to deal with the question of meaning.

W.W.: Do you take the initiative in raising the question of the

*meaning of a life-long marriage or do you wait for it to be brought
up by the people you are talking to?*
W. Gädeke: The battle is half-won if the question about the
sense and meaning of marriage can be raised at all. Men, in
particular, are usually not able—unless they are already
involved in a process of developing spiritually—to inquire
into the meaning of life or of marriage. However, if one
succeeds in raising this question concerning the point of
marriage, and when the people involved start searching for
such a meaning, a great deal will have been accomplished.

There was one case in my practice where the people had
nothing to do with anthroposophy or the Christian Community. They had come from the country via the counselling service of the Protestant Church. Talking things over,
these two very quickly reached the point of admitting to
themselves that they had no idea why they were married. In
that way the question of meaning came up very quickly.

Then I asked them both to try and order and clarify the
values they held dear in their lives, their wishes, their hopes
and expectations of life, their aims and ideals. They were
still getting on well enough with each other to look for these
things together. Then they each drew a kind of tree; it was
their own idea: what are the roots, what's the solid core, and
what should the flowers look like?
W.W.: *The tree as symbol of their marriage?*
W. Gädeke: Yes, and they positioned their values onto this
tree which symbolized their marriage. It was fascinating. I
was able to observe the different ways in which the man
and the woman approached this. Both of them had so much
creativity in them that they only came back for counselling
another two or three times and then everything was fine for
them; they were able to deal with the question of meaning
out of their own resources so purposefully that things
began to move again very quickly. Of course, this was an
exception; normally things don't work quite as smoothly as
that. In many cases a lot of work is needed before there is

any conscious recognition of the fact that marriage is not a circumstance of nature but a cultural deed, an accomplishment. And for any cultural deed to be successful you need to know why you wanted it in the first place.

W.W.: *Have you, in fact, ever come across people who were able to clearly set out their idea of marriage in response to your question?*

W.Gädeke: There have been people who were able to express it very tentatively. But I have never met a case where a couple was able to encompass the moral intuition of marriage completely by themselves, without help. It is very difficult. But there are people — and I also notice this in my marriage courses — who definitely sense the direction in which it needs to go, in the sense Goethe expressed: 'At the bottom of his heart, a good person knows perfectly well what is right'. One has to wrestle for the clear expression of the idea.

When the man is stuck ...

W.W.: *Let's take another example: A couple, married for ten years, the children are just starting school. The woman encounters anthroposophy through the Waldorf school and develops enthusiasm for it, but the man, on account of his more rigid inner life, is totally inflexible with regard to these things. The door is wide open for marriage problems. What do you advise?*

W. Gädeke: First of all a piece of advice to the woman: refrain from trying to convert your man with your own enthusiasm; don't even contemplate it! To speak about matters anthroposophical only when asked is something women find terribly difficult because their own enthusiasm tends to drive them to want to convince the man at all costs. However, the way a woman finds anthroposophy and connects with it is usually totally different from the way of a man.

A man must find his own independent path towards

things like that. The search for anthroposophy is one of those paths which must be followed on absolutely individual terms, through one's 'I' and not out of concern for the relationship, i.e. because the female partner has become involved with anthroposophy or Waldorf education. The most one could expect is that the man says: 'Fine, I will have a look at it because it interests you and because you find it fulfilling.' No more than that! It's a fact that one's own sense of being deeply moved, one's fulfilment and conviction with regard to matters of the spirit can never be transferred. Or else there will be bad blood in the marriage!

But when a marriage does run into the problem you describe it will be a time of real crisis as the man will always feel—somewhere below the surface—that the woman has acquired a soul content which he cannot share, and which might be more important even than his own soul content. For a man that's very difficult to bear.

W.W.: So how can things progress for two people in such a situation? Let's assume that the woman sticks with anthroposophy and develops further, even succeeds in not wanting to convert her partner, and the man nevertheless remains inflexible and refuses to become interested in anthroposophy. But they decide to approach you for marital counselling. What possibilities are there for the man to find some contact with anthroposophy after all? Or will it be the man's continuous blockheadedness that breaks the marriage?

W.Gädeke: Of course, such things happen; however, the man's willingness to seek marriage counselling suggests a willingness to find a common path. But for him the decisive question will be: Is he able and willing to inquire into the meaning of life? That ultimately means: does he want to raise himself towards the spirit or not? After all, questions of meaning are always questions about the spirit. Meaning will never be found in what is related to the body and the soul.

If the man takes on the question of meaning, there is a

definite way forward, and it doesn't have to be anthroposophy that is sought for. These people from the country, with the tree as a symbol of their marriage, they had nothing to do with anthroposophy, but they did have a sense for the different levels of meaning. If people don't reach the point of raising the question of shared values which is connected with the meaning sought for, the marriage cannot survive in the long term; that's my experience.

'... then all you can do is part'

W.W.: But it's also conceivable that the man presents himself for counselling because his wife wants him to and not because he considers your counselling good therapy for his marriage. I imagine you would try and find out whether the man has ever thought about the question of the meaning of marriage...?

W.Gädeke: Yes, I would try and establish whether he is able to take on such a question, whether there is any kind of resonance. If there is nothing, and if this persists, well, then nothing can be done!

W.W.: What do you say in a case like that?

W.Gädeke: Then I say to the woman that she will probably have to suffer through this and that she is unlikely to prosper in this marriage, with this man. If she finds herself able to endure it the man will still have a chance to open himself towards spiritual questions at some time, for example, by acknowledging that his children are doing well in the Waldorf school. For some men things like a parents' festival, an exhibition of children's yearly work or an active involvement in building-up a Waldorf school can provide the decisive experience that's needed. As a rule men are not so interested in the entirety of ideas connected with Waldorf education, but rather find some access through practical activity or with the help of things to look at. If however this access cannot be facilitated by any means whatsoever, life at home is likely to become a form of hell in the long run.

W.W.: *Would you advise a woman in that kind of situation to file for divorce?*

W. Gädeke: It depends, for in most cases women will want to try everything possible to cope with the situation. But there comes a point, if the man remains completely stuck, when the woman will say: 'All I do is give and give and give, it's draining me and making me ill, I cannot stand it any more'. In that case I would of course advise her: 'Either something moves in your partner, or I would advise you to separate.'

I had such a case recently, both of them were farmers, and the man was so completely stuck that there was no possibility for anything to shift: 'All you need to do is to behave in a way that is useful for our farm, then everything will be fine,' he told her. I had to say to them: 'Then all you can do is part.'

W.W.: *What did he say then?*

W. Gädeke: He was totally indignant that a priest should talk like this. I replied: 'You may find it strange that I as a priest should talk like this, but I cannot see any other way for you.' Then I heard that they went to the Protestant counselling service and that he is suddenly prepared to listen. Probably my saying that parting was the only option for them gave him such a shock that he opened up in a certain way. It doesn't matter that he is not coming to me now for counselling – the fact that he has entered into such a process in the first place is already a step towards transformation.

W.W.: *Let's take another example: A couple, married for 30 years, they hate each other's guts, are violent, have sunk into a morass of television and alcohol; a divorce is out of the question because they are so dependent on one another that neither could make it on their own.*

W.Gädeke: Couples like that don't appear in my practice

and therefore I cannot answer this question in concrete terms. If someone does come to me, that's part of his destiny, too; it means that somehow he feels that this odd priest from the Christian Community might have something to say on the subject of marriage. It means that people feel somehow that there is something spiritual involved. People who have no sense of that—however dim that sense may be—do not come to me.

W.W.: *But if a third party, say a relative of this couple, asked you for advice how to help these people?*

W.Gädeke: I would try my best, of course, but for the couple you described not a lot can be done.

W.W.: *Could one go as far as saying that it would be better for such a marriage to break up to give both partners the chance to wake up once more in this life?*

W.Gädeke: Maybe it would be better but it is impossible to say this in general terms; one would also have to look at the individual case in hand.

However, to finalize this aspect of our discussion: From time to time I do advise people to go on their separate ways. I also say then that there is nothing more I can contribute. As a rule that happens at two junctures: when the man proves unable to raise himself to the question of the meaning of marriage or when the woman has already broken out of the relationship. Even if both of the partners deal with the question of meaning—I have come across that—because both are anthroposophists, it might still be the case that nothing can go forward because the woman has already entered into a new relationship, including sexual relations. In such cases, when a woman has built up a new sexual relationship to a second man outside of the marriage, and it wasn't just a one-off but a regular thing, I have found that the woman, on account of the intensity of her new relationship, is no longer sufficiently free for open marriage counselling with the possible objective of renewing the old marriage.

The five general problems in marriages

W.W.: To conclude this theme could you summarize the five main problems affecting marriages?

W. Gädeke: a) First of all it is problematic that there is no systematic knowledge of the different sexes, no conception of the different configuration of the four members of the human being in relation to man and woman;

b) secondly, there is a lack of a concrete idea of marriage – people strive for something and seek to put it into practice without knowing what it is and how to go about it;

c) one fundamental problem, and this is not an individual one, is that there is no preparation, no training for marriage;

d) the question of sexuality which more or less follows on from the first point is a problem in itself as it bears within it the character of Chronos devouring his own children. We totally lack instruction regarding the whole issue of gender and ego. As sexual beings we are gender beings and as human beings we are supposed to be ego-beings. This is a real polarity and the problems inherent in it play into every marriage. It is such a crucial issue that I list it separately in addition to the point relating to the male and female configuration of the members;

e) and finally the question of world view and religion, the relationship to the spirit, to questions of meaning – so that one may recognize the strong repercussions of values and ideas in everyday life. Whatever is not raised into consciousness in this realm will raise its ugly head in everyday life. We have no idea how many marital problems have something to do with the fact that the question 'Henry, where do you stand with respect to religion?' was not put at the right time.

These are the five main problems which are supra-individual.

W.W.: There are some more questions I would like to raise in relation to the cultivation of marriage, as we did not deal with this very exhaustively in the first interview. Let's assume a married couple who is willing to do what they can to care for the marriage, to cultivate it. What would you advise them specifically? In order to follow up on what you've already referred to, what should they read together, what should they discuss, and for how long, how often, alone or with others?

W.Gädeke: A lot depends on how accustomed the partners are to lead any kind of a spiritual life. There are some who don't have a clue what I am referring to when I say 'spirit' and others that ask me straight away for a specific meditation. The span is very wide indeed. First of all I have to sound out individually what the possibilities are. A first step would be, for example, that they read fairy-tales together. There are also books like *Mit Märchen im Gespräch* ['Conversing with fairy-tales'] by Rudolf Geiger which encompass a gentle transition from the pictorial to the thought element, where the spiritual is taken from the imagination to the conceptual.

If the partners are scientists I might advise them to read *The Philosophy of Spiritual Activity*[7] by Rudolf Steiner and work through it together. If they are very religious people I would refer them to Emil Bock's writings.

There are countless variations, and it is always a question of personal perception; furthermore the intuition of the moment and the question of what suggests itself by their personalities plays a great part in what I might recommend.

W.W.: Could you please explain how this reading together by the marriage partners might be put into practice?

W.Gädeke: It is very important that both of them fully acknowledge that the other is reading something that is not derived from his or her own thinking, that he or she is expressing something which derives its objective nature from the very fact that it sprang from someone else's thoughts. So it is not a direct expression of the partner's soul but, in going beyond, leads in the direction of the spirit; I hear the other partner read out something or speak about something which is more than his own soul content.

There are cases where I advise doing nothing but read to one another. When they have progressed a little I might suggest, for example: 'Take turns reading the text to one another and tell each other what thoughts and feelings come up for you, but don't discuss these, just listen to the other partner telling you what effect the text has had on him. Having absorbed the objective–spiritual content, go on to receive the reflection of that spiritual content in the other's soul.'

W.W.: *In other word, listen without commentary to what the other says, without adding your own thoughts?*

W.Gädeke: Only listening, no commenting, no discussing! It's a good idea to take turns reading aloud, with both partners describing their thoughts and feelings about the passage they read. This doesn't have to be done every day, once or twice a week should be sufficient.

To people even more advanced one could say: 'Consider the view-point of the other carefully, try to describe his view-point as well as the feelings that it arouses in you! And then try to objectify each other's view-points in relation to the problem at issue, in order to really engage with the other.' Generally this is immensely difficult between a man and a woman but it is one way of entering into a proper exchange in spirit.

Participating in the other's soul content

W.W.: *And then there are the soul experiences, as discussed in the first interview. Many people reading this will say: 'We are doing that anyway, we go to concerts, we watch sunsets together, but it doesn't do much for our marriage.' What is the matter in cases like this? Is there something else lacking?*

W.Gädeke: If they enjoy the countryside together and listen to concerts they may rightly say: 'We are doing that!' because in doing so they form a community in soul. But community in soul alone is not enough to sustain a marriage, it is only one building block; in other words, even if the community of soul is taken care of in the right way the other problems we have addressed can still persist.

The essential point is allowing mutual participation in each other's soul content. Let's assume a traditional division of roles — man at work and woman at home with the children. How interested is the man really in what the woman has experienced in the day with the children? Let us assume, for instance, that the children are still small. How great is the man's interest in the child's development, the little steps it has taken, how far is he able to share the woman's delight when the child sat up for the first time? What opportunities are there to really share in the worries and woes of the other partner? Maybe the woman's mother is ill. How and in what manner does she tell him? How does he react? How do they both manage to participate in the other's individual destiny?

Or put it another way: on which occasions does one regularly speak together about the mundane matters of everyday life? Men tend to have less of a need to do this, women much more so.

W.W.: What are the most favourable occasions for this kind of exchange? Every day during lunch?

W.Gädeke: Lunch is not the best occasion. It might be possible to arrange a tea break in the afternoon, ten to fifteen minutes or so. One sits down together, drinks coffee or tea and starts talking; or else one has a hot drink together in the evening before going to bed and has a little chat. It doesn't have to be very long and detailed as long as there is some partaking of what is in the other's soul.

W.W.: And during those conversations one ought to share whatever is going on inside one at the time?

W. Gädeke: Yes. But it's important to distinguish between what can be simply related and what needs to be discussed. The latter should not be brought up on such occasions, because it requires more time; one should just aim at an exchange of matters which are not of earth-shattering significance. That's the point: to speak about things which are not earth-shattering.

Between tenderness and sex

W.W.: I would like to come back to the point you made about 'experiencing tenderness and sex as life processes as opposed to soul and body processes' (pages 26–28 and 72)

W.Gädeke: The way one deals with sexuality is, of course, of decisive importance. The problematic side of sex has nothing to do with the physical-etheric process but rather with the fact that this process is accompanied by desire. Desire is a soul force in which antipathy is stronger than sympathy (see Rudolf Steiner's *Theosophy*, in the chapter 'The Soul World'). Once you have understood that desire is in fact something which destroys love, the question arises as to how far one manages to free one's sex life from this quality of desire. Whether it is successful is another question.

W.W.: In other words, dampen down sexuality?

W.Gädeke: No, this is the crux of the matter, for in sexuality our physical-etheric nature is tightly bound up with our soul nature. The physical act of giving oneself, of pouring oneself out towards the other, of opening oneself is, as such, a gesture of love, of warmth, of devotion. It is a definite gesture of loving! However, it is perpetually torpedoed by the desire to possess, in that one basically only perceives one's own physical state. Therefore it is important to strive towards making the physical encounter a bridge to the other being, to the soul of the other.

W.W.: *Could you describe this in more detail?*

W. Gädeke: One realistic possibility would be to tone down, as far as possible, the astral element of movement in the entire act. The quieter the act of sexual union is, the more soulful it can be, and the greater will be the chance of a human encounter. On the other hand, the more passionately the whole thing is conducted, the more caught-up one is in oneself. Of course, today this can only be partially achieved, but it is possible to make efforts in this direction.

In addition we have to consider that the sense of touch *per se* is not able to perceive the world outside but only the changes the world outside brings about on or in our bodies. The sense of hearing, on the other hand, is a spiritual sense, because through my ears I really hear the entire being of the resounding body, with my eyes I only see the surface of objects, I don't see right inside them, and in the case of nose and tongue something of the other substance has even to disappear within me, that means, there is an inherent gesture of antipathy.

W.W.: *You regard the act of taking something into oneself as a gesture of antipathy?*

W.Gädeke: The act of closing off denotes antipathy, the act of separating from the world, which is necessary to take possession of something, of taking it into myself, and taking it away from the world. Sympathy denotes an act of connecting myself with the world. But as soon as I inhale something, say the scent of a rose, it remains in me and is lost to the world. I rob it, I make it my private possession, there is a quality of antipathy there.

When I touch something I merely notice the effect of the body I am touching on my own body — this is the way the sense of touch operates in physical terms. I perceive the differing states of my own body. And on account of the fact that sexual activity primarily works via the sense of touch, it has this inherent problem that we are closing ourselves off from the very thing we want to perceive: the other person.

We want to actively transcend the barriers erected by the sense of touch to get through to the other. It is possible to practise this in the context of kissing and cuddling because things are far simpler then; that's why I pointed to this aspect of tenderness in the interview about sexuality.

Religion is fundamental to the care of a marriage

W.W.: That corresponds to what was stated under point 4 (page 72). Now it would be good to elaborate to what extent the 'cultivation of a shared religious life' (see point 3, page 72) can contribute to strengthening and transforming the life-forces.

W. Gädeke: It's relatively difficult to explain this in a few words. Rudolf Steiner described in *The Education of the Child* and in *Occult Science*[8] that the religious processes – prayer, reverence, adoration etc. – are the most potent means of spiritualizing, purging and strengthening the life forces. For that reason a religious life within the marriage is such an important means of caring for the marriage, because in the absence of religious endeavour all the personal and general imperfections and difficulties of human life get bound up in the merging life forces of the partners. Hence it must be a declared aim in marriage to work towards purification of the life forces. Religion is one of the most powerful ways of all; also art, but religion even more so.

W.W.: So people who are not able to be active in conducting a religious life will be lacking something essential?

W.Gädeke: Most definitely! They don't notice it in the short term, but only in 30, 40 years' time. Whether it will then occur to them that their problems come from want of a religious life is another matter, because in this case there is a huge gap between cause and effect. But this is the reason why we are free in this realm – because we don't notice what we are doing to ourselves if we don't cultivate a religious life.

The difficulties of woman and man in grasping the idea of marriage

W.W.: In order to really grasp the idea of marriage one has to take a step back from oneself, one must have developed the consciousness soul to a certain extent and be capable of thinking objectively. In our first interview we established that men find this easier to do because of their female etheric body, while women are more strongly caught up in their constitution and therefore generally find it harder to grasp an idea — maybe some women cannot manage it at all — because they relate everything to their own nature.

If that's the case, how can a woman attain to an objective understanding of the marriage idea? After all, understanding the idea is of paramount importance to the marriage! So how does a woman acquire the ability to grasp the idea if she doesn't understand it and what does a man do if the woman proves incapable of grasping the idea?

W.Gädeke: If the man is able to fully understand the idea of marriage, it may well be that the woman is still so strongly caught up in her soul nature that she refuses, through fear of the abstract, to confront these very personal questions in the form of ideas. But if, in spite of that, she finds it within herself to agree with the content of the idea — and as a rule she is perfectly able to do just that, even more so than a man because of her stronger inclination to the spirit — she will be able to attain to the idea of marriage in another way; and the man, through his understanding of the idea, can try to mediate it to the woman in pictorial form.

If this doesn't work the two should perhaps approach a priest; he should be able to find ways and means of communicating the idea of marriage to the woman; maybe by religious pictures, maybe in another more soul-oriented way, perhaps even by way of myths so that the woman with her stronger soul nature really understands what is meant. If both are of good will the only question is in what form the idea appears; it can also be done in artistic form.

W.W.: But not every woman who cannot grasp an idea in terms of pure thinking will find access to the idea of marriage by means of the more religious or artistic route you described. After all she might — and this is surely not rare, and not rare for men either — totally refuse even to entertain the idea that it might be conducive to human evolution if two people work together to create something new, for example a new androgynous human being, or whatever.

W.Gädeke: Then the man has to ask himself whether she is the right woman for him. When the issues referred to have assumed central importance for him, when he has realized the worth of raising these issues, it may be better just to be friends with the woman concerned at first. Why on earth not? It's surely fine to say, with all the love in the world: I believe that we are not yet ready for marriage. That's not dishonourable, is it?

W.W.: How does the man accomplish the transition from objectively grasping the idea to living it in a human and soul-imbued manner? He may well be more disposed to grasping the idea, but very often the human side will be found lacking and the idea remains an abstraction! What can a man do to lead it out of the abstract? How can he learn to lead it over into real life?

W.Gädeke: That's the epitome of caring for the marriage and also of living your life altogether. How can an ideal, an idea, be turned into concrete reality? What are the steps involved? It's not a specific problem of the male, it is a general human problem, and it would go too far to try and cover this in detail here.

W.W.: Surely part of it is not to be in servitude to the idea, but confront it experientially as Rudolf Steiner describes in The Philosophy of Spiritual Activity.

W.Gädeke: It is essential to develop a living experience of the idea, again and again. One has to make effort after effort to individually and jointly grasp the idea in a living way, or else it will slip through one's spiritual fingers.

The idea of marriage: a summary

W.W.: Let us summarize what is meant by the 'idea of marriage'. In the previous interview we addressed the following: learning to balance out the one-sided aspects of the male and female nature; appreciating and loving one's partner for their different nature and striving to learn about it in order to understand its one-sided aspects; learning to love; marriage as an accomplishment of culture; creating a new 'androgynous human being'. I would like to deal with the issues of connecting to the higher group souls separately. Is there anything else?

W.Gädeke: Yes, maybe that one learns to live with the imperfections of the other and with those aspects of their nature that resist transformation.

The effect of a marriage on the life of a society

W.W.: In the context of the 'marriage idea' I would like to take up once more the aspect of 'marriage as cultural deed'. In our first interview on marriage you said that one has to practise in the smaller context what humanity needs as a whole. In what way does it affect one's fellow human beings if this way of practising flourishes? It would surely not be good enough if any expectations in this realm manifested in bizarre postulations, such as demanding of others what one is unable to achieve oneself; if it was expected of a priest, for example, that his marriage must not fail – for that would be an anti-social pressure! I am asking what effects a successful marriage has on the social conditions of humanity, and likewise a rotten marriage?

W.Gädeke: The significance of marriage really has to do with this marriage ideal, according to which human beings express the importance to their individual path of joining their lives together. If individual people succeed in transcending the deep abyss of the division of the sexes, in living in community without engaging in battle or fleeing, a major step has been accomplished.

In terms of evolving our humanity we no longer have the luxury of fighting or fleeing. And whether at the end of the century we shall be standing at the grave of civilization or be engaged in the battle of all against all, in other words, whether it will come to pass that anti-social instincts get the upper hand totally — all that will largely depend on the state of marriage, initially as an example and microcosm. However, it is an ideal of the future that more and more people learn to live in the smallest social unit without battle or flight. Every single sound marriage serves as a building-stone for this — the question will be, of course, how many building-stones there are and whether they will be sufficient for the marriage ideal to spread. This ideal has to be practised on a small scale at least.

I am looking at the piece of ground out there where a lawn has been sown; thousands of grass seeds. If only one or the other germinates here and there it will never become a lawn, but if whole patches of lawn start growing here and there they may grow together in time. Maybe that's a picture!

W.W.: But it remains in the realm of 'marriage as an example'.

W.Gädeke: Sure, but an example or model has, after all, the important function that it can engender a slowly growing certainty in those beholding it that it can be achieved in principle; in the fashion of Franz Alt's title for his book *Frieden ist möglich* ['Peace is Possible']. The mere knowledge that in marriage you are not chasing a chimera, but that, in principle, it is possible, invests the example, the model, with meaning. For it encourages others to say to themselves: 'Yes, it is possible.' Peace can be learned. Marriage can be learned. That gives rise to hope, and this is the all-important point in this field, for if we do not manage to bring it about in the small realm of marriage, how can we ever hope to achieve it on the large scale, with the enormous abysses between races, constitutions and nations?

A consciously conducted marriage has spiritual repercussions

W.W.: Could we take this a step further? What are the etheric and astral effects of a bad marriage on the world outside? How does a marriage affect the cherry trees in the garden, the geography of life forces, the earth, the souls of other people and spiritual beings overall? Are there real forces streaming into the world out of a marriage?

W.Gädeke: I have no concrete knowledge of this but I am convinced that good forces issue forth from an exemplary marriage. I cannot prove whether this enhances the growth of cherry trees but I suspect it does! First of all, it works into the world of human beings, also into the world of elemental beings and of angels. That's perfectly evident, they simply have a stronger interest in a well-conducted marriage. But the devils, too, because they want to prevent just that. As soon as I begin to conduct my marriage with a higher degree of consciousness I have to reckon with more attacks from that side. Surely that's as plain as a pikestaff! I mean the fact that I call up movement, commotion in the spiritual world, maybe even battles...

W.W.: ... when a marriage is conducted well and with a high degree of awareness?

W.Gädeke: Yes, I'm certain of this. If I was a devil I would pounce with relish on those who are doing fine. And the devil is far cleverer than I am so he has thought of it long ago.

W.W.: There is this spiritual law of evolution, isn't there, as is elaborated in the Old Testament, for example, where it is stated that Sodom and Gomorrah wouldn't have perished if there had been ten people of faith. What sort of law is that? Can it be applied today to marriage? Can one say that there must be a certain number of intact marriages in order to call forth a spiritual effect?

W. Gädeke: I would think that there is a lot of truth in that. The enigmatic thing is that Rudolf Steiner always put it like this: There has to be 'a sufficient number of people' in order for a certain positive effect to be called forth.

W.W.: How big?

W.Gädeke: Well, this is something we'd all love to know, but we shouldn't restrict our efforts to counting the number of marriages, but rather do whatever we can so that as many people as possible learn how to conduct a marriage. Our civilization is pretty good at counting, but I think that in this case it is best left to the angels for they know exactly how much a 'sufficient number of human beings' is.

Making a connection with progressive angelic beings

W.W.: In Rudolf Steiner's lectures Die Welträtsel und die Anthroposophie[9] *and* The Influence of Spiritual Beings Upon Man[10] *Rudolf Steiner speaks about human communities who are freely able to raise themselves up to an idea, and that higher group souls make a connection with such communities. What kind of entities are these?*

W.Gädeke: According to Rudolf Steiner these are progressive angelic beings, but not yet archangels. They are angeloi who are no longer allocated to individual human beings as guardian spirits but have already evolved to a stage of being able to lead small groups of people. However, they are not like the earlier group souls which worked through the blood, but are dependent on the free and voluntary streaming together of human feelings and thoughts. If this is brought about by human beings in freedom, these progressive angelic beings may unite with such a group of people and contribute whenever these people get together, when they live, strive and work together. This can happen in very different scenarios, such as the college of teachers in a Waldorf school, a group of the Anthroposophical Society or a congregation of the Christian Community.

In line with ancient Christian belief each congregation has its own angel who is symbolized by the bishop, as it were, as leader of the congregation. This notion is not that novel but what is novel about Rudolf Steiner's indication is that these entities may only work in settings where people have united out of their own free will in order to strive for an ideal.

W.W.: *Does the same apply to marriage?*

W.Gädeke: Yes, in earlier times such group spirits, also called family spirits,[11] worked instinctively in a marriage without the human beings having to contribute anything extra. Today a family spirit is only called onto the scene if people let their thoughts and feelings resonate together out of their own free will. This eventually leads—and that is the enigma—to an acceleration of the earth's spiritualization.

W.W.: *This takes place whenever a group of people who resolve to work together out of their free resolve, calls upon these beings?*

W.Gädeke: Yes, and if they are not called upon—though this is not restricted to this lifetime but is valid until the end of the earth—if by the end of the earth people have not managed to establish a connection with any of these free group souls then the human being will degenerate to an elemental being of the very worst kind. In other words, the downfall of the individual human being is, as it were, pre-programmed if, in the course of future evolution, he fails to become part of communities in which such a new free group soul works.

W.W.: *The exclusively individual path is no longer possible for man in the future? Only the path of working individually within communities?*

W.Gädeke: That's right.

W.W.: *So do two marriage partners have a higher angelos, in addition to their individual guardian angel, who establishes a connection with them? How do these three angels work together? What do you think this third angel might additionally accomplish?*

Can this angel contribute something to the marriage that cannot be brought about by the individuals concerned?

W.Gädeke: This angelos engenders community. For when I live alone I am also connected with an angel, but not with such a community angel. These community angels obviously have the possibility of working even more deeply into the entire configuration, the constituent members of the human being, because the higher the rank of an hierarchical being the more deeply it can work into man. But I cannot be any more specific as I am not aware whether Rudolf Steiner has given any more precise information about the exact potential of such group souls; but it is certain to be a penetrating effect into the social realm.

W.W.: *Is it not so that this connection with these higher angeloi as new group souls is the purpose and meaning of marriage?*

W.Gädeke: Yes, because it leads beyond individual concerns and, one may say, enables one to work towards the further evolution of the earth and other higher aims. Certainly—this is one of the most sublime purposes imaginable.

The creation of a new androgynous human being

W.W.: *In the first interview about marriage we spoke about the division of the sexes, and now it would be good to discuss the overcoming of this division as an ideal for the future. When people conduct a marriage in full consciousness of that future orientation we discussed, a new androgynous human being can be evolved with the help of spiritual beings. What is it that is evolved there? In which part of human nature does the substance of androgynous man live?*

W.Gädeke: It is indicated in the Gospel that a new heaven and a new earth will have evolved when our present earth and our present heaven will have passed away, and that there will be neither man nor woman any more. This is an outlook on the future state of the human being, in which the division of the sexes that, according to the Bible, was only a secondary deed of creation, will have been overcome again. There is not a great deal more said about it in the New Testament. However, Rudolf Steiner speaks exhaustively about overcoming the merely masculine and the merely feminine, i.e. the division of the sexes. He also speaks about the end of the current form of procreation: even in a relatively near future the human body will have been transformed — and with it all of nature — in such a way that everything will be following the course of greater and greater spiritualization, but only in the case of people who have united with the Christ. The resurrective power of the Christ will then be working in the bodily nature of man as a transforming and spiritualizing power.

W.W.: How is this prepared here and now? Are there already features in human nature that may be attributed to this evolving androgynous man, for example in the context of marriage, the partners' striving to overcome their respective one-sidedness?

W.Gädeke: As we discussed in the first interview, the division of the sexes is not just a bodily-physical fact but also concerns the life and soul forces; hence it follows that any form of human striving towards overcoming the sharp contrast between man and woman in the soul realm, and later also in the etheric realm, will prepare the overcoming of the division of the sexes in the realm of the physical. But this deed of overcoming must be accomplished from top to bottom, as it were, from the spirit via the soul nature to the life forces and finally the physical nature. It always starts on the level of the spirit; this is where the overcoming of the division of the sexes is already beginning today, everywhere indeed where human beings strive to perfect their soul lives beyond the barriers of their male or female polarization.

W.W.: Are there any indications by Rudolf Steiner about whether and how the fruits of one's efforts towards this aim in this life are carried over into a subsequent life?

W.Gädeke: Everything that can happen in terms of such a conscious transformation of the members of soul and body through the human 'I' – a transformation striven for out of one's freedom and insight as an individual in contrast to changes enforced by cultural conditions – all the products of such transformation of our constituent members remain with the human 'I' after death. By virtue of their spiritual nature they become part of the individuality's continued existence, they don't have to dissolve. In short, all that is genuinely striven for and accomplished remains permanent in the human being.

W.W.: And what will this new androgynous human being be like when it comes into being one day?

W.Gädeke: There are some indications of Rudolf Steiner that are very hard to accept with our contemporary understanding, for instance when he says that future procreation will come to pass by language and the larynx, indeed by the male larynx. The larynx is going to develop into an organ of reproduction. I challenge anyone to understand this. It's really difficult!

But he also says that today's sexual organs are the last to have evolved and will be the first to disappear, the first to become rudimentary. There are signs of this already today – in our civilized countries infertility is one of the overriding problems in this field.

Married couples in larger communities

W.W.: How does a couple in an intact marriage and with a powerful etheric sheath around them affect others in a larger type of community? Does a fertilizing element issue forth from them?

W.Gädeke: That depends on how these people place themselves in that community. Such a couple can be a crystallizing focus for a larger community. But it's equally possible that such a couple becomes, by virtue of its strong community of life forces, habits etc., a real hindrance for the other members of a larger community. For example, if one couple takes on a strong and determining role in a small Waldorf college of teachers, respresenting one force, one conviction, as it were, this can form a real blockade against others finding their way into the community.

W.W.: *What effect does such over-emphasis have? Is it to do with the shared etheric sheath?*

W. Gädeke: I would say that it's rather a question of the constellation. If there is a sufficient number of others able to provide a counterweight it need not have negative repercussions at all. However, if both claim a leading role the others will hardly get a leg on board.

Such a thing can also lead to problems, of course; in Christian Community congregations for example, when there is a priest couple and only one or two other priests besides.

But it doesn't have to be a problem. However, the smaller the circle of people wanting or doing something together, the more difficult it will be if a couple fulfils a certain task in it. When the one partner carries this and the other that responsibility it's not so difficult, but if they carry the same responsibility in the same sphere of work it can become very tricky.

W.W.: *Is this the reason why Rudolf Steiner addressed his second wife, Marie Steiner, in a most peculiar way in public?*

W.Gädeke: It's conceivable that it played a part when Rudolf Steiner always referred to and addressed his wife as 'Frau Doktor' in public, which is bound to strike some of us as a bit peculiar today. I imagine that in doing so he simply established the soul-spiritual fact of there being a difference in their joint work, in spite of the fact that their cooperation was intense and close. Maybe it also made it easier for those around them to deal with these outstanding personalities.

Children in broken marriages

W.W.: You mentioned already that children are not there to give meaning to lifelong monogamy. Would it be advisable to carry on a broken marriage because of the children?

W.Gädeke: The fact that there are children ought to give rise to the partners asking themselves whether it is possible to conduct the marriage, but does not provide the reason for doing so.

W.W.: Let's assume that the marriage was going reasonably well, children came along, the marriage started to founder soon after and the couple would separate if it weren't for the children. Should they stay together for the sake of the children?

W.Gädeke: Staying together *just* for the children's sake places an enormous strain on the children's destiny; it would be far better to find ways, maybe with the help of marital counselling, to re-establish the marriage. If people cling to the idea of staying together for the children's sake the children are overtaxed in their very existence, because in this case they have to prop up, to support the marriage. But the marriage ought to be the children's support. For that reason it is always unfortunate if chilren are the *only* reason for a couple staying together.

W.W.: When a couple separates while the children are very small still, is it advisable to take a radical step, i.e. let the children be with one of the partners until puberty, or should they commute back and forth?

W.Gädeke: I have revised my views on this question since I have been acquainted with the expertise and findings of numerous people who have gone through such situations as well as family therapists.[12] I would put it like this: it does further the children's development to have regular contact to the separate parent if the parents mutually recognize and acknowledge their differences (also in the way they bring up the children) and totally refrain from criticizing the former partner in the children's presence. This also entails listening to the children's reports after access visits without passing judgement. If this is not possible some form of family counselling involving all the parties should be sought after the separation.

W.W.: *How is it from a karmic point-of-view when one considers that the child before birth has chosen both of his parents who then separate in the child's lifetime?*

W.Gädeke: It places a heavy burden on the child's development — without any doubt! In all 'problem groups' the children of divorced parents are over-represented. Naturally the child will experience a sense of deepest disappointment and this affects the child's will to live. For in the first two seven-year-cycles — during the time when it is not yet a gender being in the real sense — the child needs both elements of humanness: the fatherly and the motherly element.

Hence divorce deprives the child of something and this will leave deep marks in his biography. Of course this does not imply that every such child is bound to become psychologically ill, but it does represent a heavy toll.

For this reason it is really appropriate, when there are children in a troubled marriage, to make the fact of the children's existence the reason for doing one's utmost to encourage a reconciliation between the two partners. However, if this proves impossible it is better to part than engage in daily warfare.

PART TWO

LECTURES

1. Man and Woman — 'The Little Difference'

Before we address the problem of marriage, I should like to place it in the context of certain realities. There are things which are normal and things which are healthy. It is healthy for someone to have 32 teeth in their mouth and no fillings. That is indeed healthy, but it is not normal. The reverse is also true: if 98 per cent of people have caries then it is certainly normal but not healthy. The situation is similar with marriage. For it is normal today that a high percentage of all marriages fail, i.e. that a lifelong partnership is not sustained; but that is not to say that it is healthy.

We shall start by tackling the fundamental problem that lies at the root of the problem of marriage — the division of mankind into male and female beings.

What does this really mean? Are we not after all primarily human beings? Don't we all, seen physically, have a head, arms, legs and a trunk? Are our internal organs not basically the same? Thus one can ask the question how it can seem justifiable at all to highlight these differences between man and woman, between male and female beings. Is it not just this that *causes* the problem?

In the distant past it was taken for granted that one experienced the masculine and feminine principles as fundamental opposites, as a universal polarity. Just consider the Chinese philosophy of Yin and Yang which explains the whole world, the whole cosmos, the entire world process in terms of the polarities of male and female, their struggling and working together. Or consider the various myths of the Greeks, Teutonic and other peoples, in which male and female deities wrestle with each other: Hera and Zeus, Athene and Mars and all the rest. It would not have occurred to the mythical consciousness of pre-philosophical human beings to try to diminish or play down the difference between male and female. On the contrary, it was perceived as being of fundamental importance to the world order. Later on a more rational consciousness tended to overlook this. Philosophical thinking, particularly in the last 200 years, gave rise to an idea whose helpfulness, indeed healthiness might be questioned. I am thinking of the concept of the equality of all human beings.

Are all human beings equal?

The idea that all human beings are equal is at first rather attractive, particularly when one considers how people have lived through the ages and how some have been oppressed and mistreated by others — not just slaves by their masters, but also women by men or vice versa, men by women. But is not the equality of men and women more of a claim, more of a postulate than a description of reality? Are we really the same?

Well we all have a nose in the middle of our face, our mouth beneath it and not above. The latter may be found, but only in Picasso's work, who re-arranged his faces. In all the essentials we are physically the same. And yet we are all very different. Is there any point in discussing the difference between woman and man, between the feminine and the masculine? Is this not something of secondary importance?

Particularly in the last 20 years representatives of the younger generation have increasingly and forcefully put the view that it is quite wrong to highlight the differences so much. It would be more helpful to focus on what people have in common. We are after all human first, man or woman second. What is so captivating about this idea is that it is so accessible, that everyone can have the feeling, 'Yes, that is right!' Eventually it became the basis for certain claims and certain habits extending right into questions of appropriate dress. Just remember the headline in *Der Spiegel*, 'The Third Sex'. In the magazine were described those interesting tendencies to progressively erode the image of what is masculine and feminine, to the extent that the same fashion, hairstyles etc. are adopted by both sexes. This would have been inconceivable some time ago! There used to be very clear rules, for instance in Joan of Arc's days: a girl does not wear trousers and does not ride a horse. It was simply not allowed!

Many such rules are so outdated that one can only rejoice that they have at last fallen by the wayside. But has the baby not been thrown out with the bath water? Despite all our similarities there are still some very fundamental differences, even at a physical level. Since marriage of whatever kind – whether monogamous, polygamous, communal or other – always has to do with the relationship of the sexes to each other, we have to consider the differences. But in what respects are we truly equal?

Let us look at ourselves: each of us looks different from his neighbour. No two men or two women are the same – apart from perhaps a few identical twins, where one may still wonder after years of knowing them how they differ. Normally we have no difficulty distinguishing one human being from another. Just because he is a man, it does not mean we have trouble telling him apart from another man. Likewise with women. What justification do we have for speaking of equality?

We know for example that a human being has his own individual protein in his physical make-up. I am thinking now of immune reactions after organ transplants. This fact is significant in that context. Right into the detail of the components of the physical body, each human being is quite individual, not just in the uniqueness of their fingerprints. Nevertheless one can still say that the structure of our physical bodies is based on a blue-print, on an idea – on the idea either of the male or the female body. The distinctions are classified as primary and secondary sexual characteristics.

But then the question arises: what importance does one attach to these distinctions? The fact of there being certain unalterable and undeniable physical differences is quite clear. A man is simply incapable of bearing and suckling a child and a woman cannot conceive a child without a man. Fundamental things like these cannot be dismissed.

Fundamental and relative differences in the male and female physique

In the last two decades feminists and other interest groups have done a great deal to clear up the issue of the difference between men and women. Alice Schwarzer was prominent among them with her book *Der Kleine Unterschied* ['The little difference']. And whilst there is considerable merit in her tirade against the rigid division of tasks in partnerships, she goes way beyond the pale when she claims that almost all or indeed all differences between men and women are socially determined or the result of their education, that they have only arisen out of the repressive mechanisms of patriarchal attitudes, which wish to preserve the domination of males. This is simply not tenable! This is ideology, not science!

It is not so long ago that the discovery was made that there is a clear genetic distinction between men and women, namely in one pair of chromosomes. Where women have two X chromosomes, men have one X and one Y chromosome – in each cell! This discovery implies that men and women are undeniably different right down to the level of each individual cell.

At the same time, a discovery was made that could virtually imply the opposite: a discovery relating to hormones, those fine substances that are emitted by the internal secretory organs or endocrine glands, the pituitary glands, the gonads, all the various hormone-secreting glands. The discovery was that whilst there are clear distinctions in these functions between men and women, all the hormones appear *both* in the male and the female organisms, albeit in different quantitative relationships and mixtures. The specific quantitative relationships of the hormones to each other are referred to as the hormone balance. Much has been written about these, oestrogens and androgens and all the rest of them. Without going deeply into it, one can say that in the female organism there is a preponderance of certain kinds of hormones and conversely, that in the male organism others predominate. This biological research has shown that on the one hand men and women are fundamentally different – having different chromosomes – and on the other hand that they are only relatively different in that the same hormones are present but in varying quantities. One could therefore say that there are differences both of degree and kind. Also that it would be equally wrong to maintain that they are absolutely different or absolutely the same. If however the sexes were considered broadly similar, and the humanity we have in common were the most influential aspect of us, then there should really not be as many problems between men and women as in fact there are.

A study of the sexes

I should like to take a closer look at the sexes, starting from a few basic facts. We all have a physical body, both men and women [*here the lecturer does an illustration on the blackboard to which he adds details during the course of the lecture*].

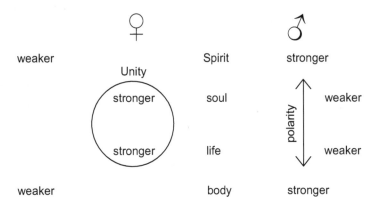

If we look at the physical body there are generally characteristic differences between men and women. The man is noticeably heavier and bigger, one could say more earthbound, than the woman. This is true in many different specific ways, such as the fact that given the same muscular weight, the man can exert 30 per cent more force than the woman. Many other phenomena point to the fact that men have more powerful, stronger and heavier bodies. So, next to 'body' here, I shall write simply 'stronger' and 'weaker'. That is no value judgement, but a mere fact.

A comparison of life-forces

Now in addition to the physical body itself, we also have within it the forces of life at work. A comparison of these gives a very different picture. One example: of all the embryos that develop in the womb after the fertilization of an ovum, there are 130 males to every 100 females. At birth the ratio falls to 106 to 100. When full adulthood is reached at around 21 the ratio evens out to 100 males to 100 females. What does this mean? It means that even at the peak of its vitality the male organism is more susceptible to disorders, much more moribund. This is reflected in a much higher death rate – the so-called perinatal mortality – after birth. The incidence of infant mortality is roughly a third higher in boys than in girls. In all problem categories among children – whether psychiatric, or involving behavioural difficulties, dyslexia or autism – boys tend to be 30–40 per cent more affected than girls, a trend which continues on into adolescence. The development of male life seems to be a great deal more complicated or a great deal more easily overcome by death.

To this one can add that life expectancy among women in the Federal Republic of Germany is currently around 10 per cent greater than for men. The latter, according to statistics published annually by the insurance industry, have a life-expectancy of around 70 years, whereas for the women it is around 77. There are always slight variations. Nevertheless one can say that life expectancy for a woman is around 10 per cent longer than for a man. If we take a look at old peoples' homes . . .

Female member of the audience interrupts: There are only women there. There are hardly any men in residential care!
Precisely: men die sooner. Women on the other hand simply dwindle away over a period of years, don't they? If you take an old people's home or a geriatric ward with up to 90 beds then you may find only about four men there. Conclusion: men die earlier. What does this mean?

It means that a woman's life forces are clearly stronger than those of a man. This is also reflected in the fact that a woman is capable – by virtue of her organism, her life forces – of bringing forth a new life out of her own, of giving shape to an organism which is so alive that it can sustain itself. This is a process that takes place over a period of months and by the time the baby is weaned can take up to one and half years. The female organism can facilitate this extraordinary achievement of the life-forces within it. By contrast the man's contribution is positively tiny, both in terms of time, energy and quantity. We can thus conclude unequivocally: in the area of vitality the relationship between 'strong' and 'weak' in man and woman is reversed.

Do men have a soul at all?

I shall just touch on another area which we might return to later on. How do things look in the realm of the soul-forces? Women will surely quickly agree if I say: sometimes one can doubt whether men have souls at all! [*Laughter among the audience.*] At any rate, what women understand by soul is something they often seek for in vain in their men. It is strange, is it not? Or is there a woman present who does not agree? [*Renewed laughter.*]

Female listener: *I actually think men are more sensitive than women.*

Even more sensitive? Or are they perhaps just more touchy? [*Signs of agreement among the audience – laughter.*] Might these two things be different? Does the man have just as much richness and abundance in his soul life as the woman?

Female listener: *I think that men are more vulnerable...*

I feel we must look a little more closely at just what that vulnerability is. Is it really vulnerability of soul? If we mean the soul with all its variety of feelings, the wealth of concepts and imagination, the wealth of memories etc... [*Female listener mentions poets and musicians.*] Of course. There are indeed many men who being artists are richly endowed with soul forces. But in ordinary human social intercourse, in what weaves between one human being and another, soul to soul, women are often left with the feeling that there could be more there. This is an area where women often feel under-nourished, as if unable to get a proper echo.

So let me just write up tentatively: the soul-life of men is simply weaker and that of women stronger: in the sense, for

example, that a woman is much more ready to admit to a mistake than a man. [*Signs of agreement and laughter.*] And also much more ready to turn to someone else and say 'Help me, please!'
Female listener: *Men certainly don't do that! [Laughter.]*
Or alternatively, simply making contacts, or even just expressing what is going on in their feeling life — these are things that men find extremely difficult. They always tend to objectify these matters and speak of them in a detached way. So we can say that the soul-life of men is basically weaker, but they tend to objectify it and speak of objective problems. There is always the tendency to depersonalize everything and to say: 'Generally this and that is the case.' By contrast 'What does it mean to me?' and 'Where am I in this?' are questions men tend to block off.

The difference in outlook

The whole of natural science has evolved on the basis that people said: 'What one feels about things, how they might strike me, whether I find them good and beautiful, whether I like them or not, is all of no importance. What matters is the thing itself.' This is precisely the attitude which Rudolf Steiner describes as a spiritual one.

If you open one of Rudolf Steiner's fundamental works, *Theosophy*, you will find in the first chapter that he makes a distinction between body, soul and spirit. The difference between soul and spirit lies precisely in the two approaches outlined above. The spiritual approach does not consist in asking questions such as: 'Do I like this green, these flowers? Is this of any use to me? Can I do anything with it?' But rather: 'Why do dahlias bloom in the autumn rather than in the spring?' Whether I like the flowers or not is a matter of complete indifference. I can get involved with them in such a way that I ask: 'What kind of laws are at work in a situation where composite flowers do not flower in spring, not in significant quantities anyway, but where mono-cotyledons — the single seed-leaf plants like the snowdrops, crocuses, tulips and daffodils — do? Why do they flower in the spring and not in the autumn?' Such questions have nothing whatever to do with my own feelings towards the flowers.

Such an approach is also one which men find much more congenial than women. Women are perhaps more inclined to say: 'I think those flowers are beautiful. I like them.' These approaches reveal a different point of view, a different outlook, and women find it generally much more difficult to disregard their own feelings about this or that object or impression. Thus we can say that men find it easier to adopt the objective spiritual point of view, while women prefer a more subjective one.

From the perspective of spiritual science, Rudolf Steiner put it this way: women live predominantly in the unity of their soul and life forces, in the unity of their astral and etheric bodies, to use those terms. Men on the other hand, live primarily in the polarity of the ego and the physical body.

Well this may be taken as an initial orientation, a screen, as it were, through which a number of things may be observed. Take for example the myth of the rib. If you can imagine that the primeval human being was both male and female, both principles interwoven, then all the above aspects of the human being would have been equally strong. Later, something is taken out of the middle of this human being and forms the basis for an independent human being of its own. The one is extended upwards and downwards to become complete (the woman) and the other is joined together in the middle (the man). There you have in picture form the very situation we have just set out: the man is lacking a certain something in the middle, is weaker in that area. He is missing a rib, in the language of the myth.

Now this should not be seen as better or worse in either case. There can be no question of making value judgements, but rather of stating the facts from a detached, male point of view; not from the female perspective of 'What does this mean for me?'

Male and female germ cells – unity and diversity

I should like to place another picture before you. Let us look at the areas in which the human being is unambiguously only male or only female. We then come to the smallest units, namely the germ cells, and they have characteristic differences. I should like to illustrate that by means of the female ovum and the male sperm. [*Draws.*]

The ovum is relatively big, just about visible, and is round and fairly inactive. It has no activity of its own, drops as it were, out of the ovaries and is propelled by the efforts of the follicles down the fallopian tube into the womb, where it is then either fertilized or passed out unfertilized at some point. By contrast the male seed is a great deal smaller. I cannot therefore draw it to scale. It has a roughly conical head and a long whip-like tail, consisting clearly of two parts, whereas the female egg is equally clearly an image of unity. The male sperm is very small, propels itself, and after copulation moves upwards on its own towards the female germ cell, the ovum.

In their form, we see at first the polarity of round and straight. Those of you who were pupils at a Steiner Waldorf school, or who have children there yourselves, will know what the pupils learn in their first lesson: the curve and the straight line, as the universal principles of Yin and Yang, one might say. Then, secondly, we have the elements of rest and movement. Thirdly we can look at their functions, at their purpose: in the case of the ovum it is to receive and conceive; it has a centripetal orientation. Something has to

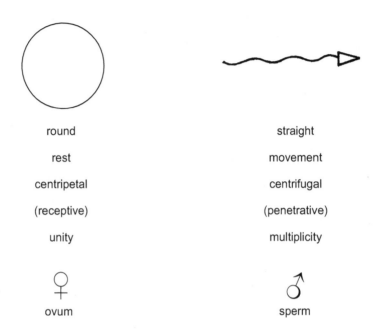

round	straight
rest	movement
centripetal	centrifugal
(receptive)	(penetrative)
unity	multiplicity
ovum	sperm

come towards it. In the case of the male seed the opposite is
true: the many spermatozoa have a centrifugal tendency.
They move of their own accord. Thus we see straightaway
that even the smallest elements of the human organism are
oriented and organized as polarities. And so we may write
underneath our illustration what I have just said: unity
(woman) and duality (man) or even unity and plurality. A
single sperm is inconceivable, it simply does not occur.
Spermatozoa always appear in vast numbers, not merely in
hundreds or thousands but in millions. Ova on the other
hand always appear singly or at most in pairs.

Rest and movement — head and limbs

A third picture emerges from the organism as a whole. If we
accept these principles as the fundamental principles of the
male and the female, then we may observe that we are all

built according to a female principle in the upper part of the human being, in the rounded spherical head. That part of us is at rest! The head is the bearer of our consciousness, essentially of our nervous system, precisely because it is organically designed to be at rest. The raising up of the human being from the animal is just the process whereby the head is liberated from the movement of the body, in particular from the grasping function of the lower jaw, which still plays a significant role among animals. Since the feet take care of locomotion, the hands are freed up to take over the grasping function. Since the hands are doing the grasping, the jaw no longer needs to. Thus the lower jaw can serve for the purpose of speech, a truly human capacity! Moreover, the head is brought out of the hanging position in which it is constantly subject to the movement of the body, into a centrally supported one, which permits the development of the brain, etc. In short, a position of rest is essential for thinking and perceiving.

You can test this yourself by swaying your head from side to side like an elephant and trying at the same time to think. [*Laughter.*] Just try it! You need only do it for half a minute and you will notice that you cannot think! And then try to work out 7×17! Or try to listen to birdsong while doing that, i.e. to carry out an exact observation. You will notice that a position of rest in this area is essential if the activities of the nerve-sense organism, perception and thinking are to go on in a human way.

The human head is entirely geared to receptivity, thoughts are apprehended, the perceptions which come in through the ears, nose and mouth, nourishment and breathing. The only exceptions are exhalation and speech, the only healthy exceptions, since if anything else comes out, the human being is ill. At the other end of the human organism we have precisely the opposite phenomena. We have no longer the unity of the head but the duality or plurality of the limbs.

Everything about this end of the human being extends out into the world. I go out into the world, I intervene in the events of the world. The same applies to the soul forces to which we shall return in a moment. At this stage we can say that the bodily shape and form is centrifugal, directed outwards, and that the limbs and the bones in them tend to be straight.

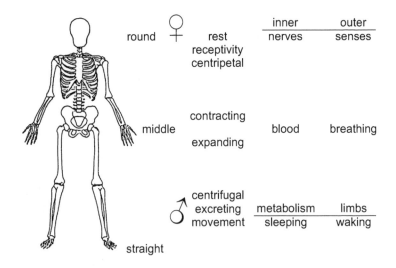

			inner	outer
round	♀	rest receptivity centripetal	nerves	senses
middle		contracting expanding	blood	breathing
straight	♂	centrifugal excreting movement	metabolism sleeping	limbs waking

Within the metabolism the natural tendency is rather towards not leaving in its prior state what has been received—as is the case with perception and thinking which can thus be objective—but rather to completely destroy the nourishment taken in, to deprive it of its own character and to use it to build up the substance of the body. Thus in the metabolic and limb system the human being makes its mark on matter and the world. That is movement, the movement of the will which finds its primary expression in the limbs. In summary we can say that we are all female in the organization of our heads and male in that of our limbs, if we take what we have observed to be the basic phenomena of the male and female organisms.

The middle realm of the human being

In between these two poles we have the middle part of the human being: chest, breathing, blood circulation. Here we have mediating functions, not only expansion and contraction but also breathing in and breathing out, systole and diastole of the heart, the blood circulation. In the breathing and in the beat of the pulse we have these two functions of movement in rhythmical interchange.

The same applies to the formative principles in the ribs for example. With the ribs we no longer have the enclosed form of the skull, no round, spherical form that is firm and at rest, but rather a rib-cage which as a whole has an approximately spherical character, but which opens up towards its lower end. The ribs become ever straighter the further down they go; at the top they are rounded and curved, further down they become more and more like limbs. Individually they are no longer round and spherical, but they are curved and together form a sphere. Occurring in a repeated pattern, they are more mobile below than above; at the top they are firm and bony, at the bottom rather softer and more cartilaginous. And there one can see the division into two parts of the middle realm of the human being, right down into the details of rib-cage formation. You will find this all wonderfully set out in a wealth of detail in the beautiful book by Lother Vogel: *Der Dreigliedrige Mensch* ['The threefold human being']. Let this be sufficient for the time being.

Inner and outer in the threefold human being

The male/female question becomes really interesting when

we look at the area in which man and woman are radically different—namely in the reproductive organs. At first glance one can say that the man is clearly oriented towards the limbs—even from the normal perspective—and stronger in his torso. The women is on the whole more likely to have rounded contours, the man straighter and more angular.

If we look beyond the soul functions (which in the head have predominantly to do with thinking and perceiving, in the metabolic and limb system with the will, and in the middle with feeling) and if we think about the states of awareness that are connected with them, then we can see that all three systems—the nerve-sense system, the rhythmic system and the metabolic limb system—each have two aspects: the rhythmic system is divided into breathing and circulation, the nerve-sense systems as the name suggests into nerves and senses and finally the metabolic-limb system into metabolism on the one hand and limbs on the other. In each system one of the parts is directed outwards: in the head the senses, in the middle the breathing and in the lower area the limbs.

In each case the other part of the system is directed inwards. The nervous system is directed inwards—not only spatially, but also functionally as an organ of the organism itself. It does not serve to make a connection with the outer world. The same applies to the blood circulation, which is healthy only so long as it is enclosed within the organism. The metabolism is also an enclosed system even to the extent of its situation within the abdomen. This does not mean that it has absolutely no connection with the outside. It does, of course, but only by way of excretion.

In terms of consciousness the key point is that the part of the organism which is directed outward is in each case the more conscious: senses, breathing, limbs. In our senses we are fully awake. We can consciously direct our senses; we can close our eyes, focus, listen, switch-off. You may have seen how a wine-taster goes about his business, sniffing, dreamily half-closing his eyes; or indeed what goes on when he takes his first sip ... seen from outside it looks incredibly funny. So we can direct our senses consciously. The activity of our nerves, on the other hand, we know nothing about – as long as they are healthy.

In the rhythmic part of my being, I can hold my breath. I can also deliberately accelerate my breathing. I can have a distinct awareness of my breathing whenever I wish. It is very different with the blood circulation.

Then in the metabolism and in the limbs it is also quite clear that I can perceive and guide the movements of my limbs, whereas in the case of my metabolism it is better if I do not know what is going on, for if I do, there is sure to be something wrong; there can be no question of my playing an active role in directing my digestion. The waking ego-consciousness can really only be active in the three areas whose natural tendency is to be directed outwards.

The male and the female reproductive systems

There follows from this something very significant about the difference between men and women. The reproductive organs which are placed between the metabolic and limb systems are in the case of a woman almost entirely contained within the frame of the body, i.e. in the area in which the human being tends to be asleep or dreaming. With a man on the other hand the reproductive organs are projected out of the metabolic area like a kind of limb, in an area in which the human being is awake and has a clear consciousness. Thus, in observing the organs of man and woman we have already a clear indication that in respect of the sex organs, the reproductive organs, men and women have completely different experiences of soul and consciousness, they are indeed polar opposites. I should elaborate a little further on this picture.

If we take a somewhat schematic look at the female and male reproductive organs, then we can see that those of the woman are in some ways more primitive, for the gonads are enclosed in the abdomen. There we find the ovaries which have an approximately spherical form, somewhat elongated but still more or less rounded, as one might expect from the female processes at work. They have a head-like form. We have seen that the head is the area in which our life processes are least present, indeed in which their opposite is to be found, namely the decomposition of life processes so that consciousness can take place. This process of decomposition in the head is expressed in the fact that the substance of the nerves is the most delicate in the body, and the most liable to die off.

The relative deadness of the organism in the head is also reflected in the female gonads in the sense that all the woman's eggs, a few hundred thousand, are already present in rudimentary form when she is born as a girl. They all remain preserved over a period of decades and do not increase or decrease in number. There is no further nuclear division, no further life process. When puberty is reached, they then ripen one after another at four-weekly intervals and fall down the fallopian tubes into the womb. Thus this is an area which is relatively dead, round, calm, lifeless.

The womb on the other hand is an organ which in many details resembles the heart. It is a muscular cavity which is designed to expand and contract, to take something in and push it out. The correlation between the womb and the heart extends right into the detail of its fibrous structure, into the detail of each muscle fibre: a central muscular cavity. Below it we have the vagina in which more radial, straight structures predominate: a kind of negative limb. Thus, from above down, we have a metamorphosis of the principles of the human, head, heart and limbs. Nevertheless the complete human being is represented.

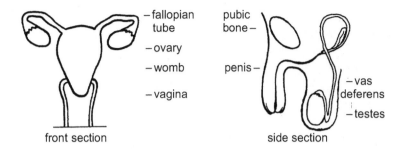

front section   side section

All this is very different in the man, by virtue of the Y chromosomes and the corresponding hormones which are produced in the embryo of the developing boy. The rudimentary uterus atrophies and the whole organism is pushed outwards as it were. The result is that the gonads come down out of the abdomen, sometimes just before, and in other cases just after birth.

The testes grow right out of the organism and what happens in them is the polar opposite to what happens in the female gonads. Whilst the ovaries are more or less permanently at rest, the testes are constantly moving. Whilst there is no further nuclear division in the ovaries, it is constantly happening in the testes. Whilst a woman's ovaries contain only 4-600,000 egg cells, of which only a few hundred actually mature during the course of her life, the man produces 120 million spermatozoa every day! 120 million! 120 million! These make their way through the ductus deferens into the organism, and out through the penis. So there you have a kind of limb which appears above the head-like formation: in other words a kind of human being the wrong way up. The upper part is turned down, and the lower part upwards.

The whole reproductive organism of the woman has the character of metabolism and in terms of her feelings is in more of a dreamlike or subconscious state; the reproductive organism of the man on the other hand has the character of the limbs, clearly has a life of its own which impinges on the waking consciousness. The middle part of the female organ, the uterus, is scarcely represented at all in the man, apart from a little cluster of cells which no longer has any significance. The man's reproductive system has no middle, and where the middle would be there is a bone.

This is yet another picture which speaks its own language. None of the foregoing is intended to represent a value judgement in any way, but simply a description of the difference between the man and the woman. The female reproductive system is embedded in the sleeping metabolic area whereas that of the man is in the waking limb area. The former appears in itself and within the organism as a kind of unit, the latter forms more of a polarity in relation to the organism as a whole.

Summary

Let us take all this a step further: in his head the man has primarily female characteristics as does the woman. In their limbs both man and woman are both primarily male in terms of the form principles at work. The reproductive organs however endow the man with an additional limb-like appendage, an additional male principle. A woman on the other hand has unequivocally female characteristics in her reproductive system, notably in the middle part of the organ. One could also say: the male principles in the lower part of the woman's body are mitigated by female qualities. In the man on the other hand, the male principle in the limbs is reinforced by the reproductive system. He is, as it were, doubly endowed with limbs.

The etheric body in man and woman

Now comes a concept which many of you may already be familiar with. Rudolf Steiner often pointed out that the life forces in the man are female and those of the woman are male. The forces that is, that build up our bodies, enliven them and enable us to grow and reproduce. Put briefly, men have female and women male etheric bodies. What does he mean? How can this be understood?

If one looks at the human organism, one can say that generally the etheric forces, the life forces of the human being are capable of producing either a male or a female body, i.e. the etheric body must be capable of both. Yet in the one case they are prevented from developing certain organs and in the other they are stimulated to do just that. This actually means that certain formative forces are not employed to produce organs in the man. In the first stages of life, in the embryo, the male has the possibility in terms of life-forces of producing either male or female organs. But after about the seventh week of pregnancy, the formative forces confine themselves to one and not the other. Then one could say the male formative forces become active and form a male reproductive system. The female formative forces therefore cannot get to work in this area. What happens to these formative forces which do not find expression in the body? Many of you will know the answer to this from your experience of children. Children do not start at Waldorf schools until they are 7. That is because this is the age at which certain formative forces are no longer required for building up the body. This is expressed in the fact that the first permanent teeth have begun to come through and that the forces that put them there are thus no longer needed to do that. These forces are thus available for the cultivation of a conscious soul-life, for the culture of learning. This fundamental concept can help us further with our considerations. For we can say that the female etheric forces which are preserved because no female physical organs are formed now stand at the disposal of a conscious soul-life. The reverse is also true, the male formative forces in a woman are prevented from developing male organs and thus become available for her soul-life, first and foremost in her thinking.

'The man's ideal is a machine'

One can put this as follows: This state of affairs underlies the fact that the male way of thinking has a double dose of the female tendency of the head, namely the tendency towards objectivity: only to recognize what is outside; only to let things come in without in any way interfering with them, representing what is in the world without the female tendency to represent what is in oneself. Male consciousness is such that the man inclines to be fanatically objective. 'But that is simply how it is. Can't you see that! Just look and you will see there is no other way it could be!' Typically male expressions. Woman do not appreciate such sentiments. For, as many of you will notice when a man has to explain something to a woman, to explain it quite objectively, she will generally respond with a 'yes' to each point. When he finishes his explanation and is delighted that he has been able to persuade her, she will suddenly say, 'But nevertheless...' [*Laughter.*] That sort of thing can drive any man up the wall! 'But I have just explained it to you! What do you mean nevertheless?'

This is because the thinking life of a woman is organized in a very different way, because male formative forces are at work in it, so that a tendency to represent one's own interests and to move of one's own accord plays in to the working of the conscious mind. Women are by no means content to leave concepts as they are but like to transform and change them. Indeed there is a constant tendency in the soul-life of a woman to change things. Women are much more inclined to change their clothes, their hairstyle, to move the furniture, to make any change of that sort because their conscious soul-life is disinclined to leave things as

they are. Perhaps the reverse is reflected in male compla-
cency: ideally everything should carry on the way it has
been set up, everything should simply work. Men incline to
want everything to work without them getting involved:
women, children, all of them should just get on with it! The
opposite is true of women, they know very well that
everything requires constant effort of will, constant initiative and care on their part.

The male ideal is the machine. [*Laughter.*] This is why
men are so fascinated by machines and can be moved to
tears when they work so well. When the V2 rocket took off
for the first time in Penemünde and flew, Wernher Von
Braun and the others flung themselves into each others
arms and wept for joy. This is something a woman can
scarcely imagine doing. She simply can't imagine feeling
the same way about it. Only men can share feelings of that
sort; and in different circumstances, when it is the women
who are weeping in each others arms, the men stand
around looking awkward and the women say: 'Can't you
see what's going on. Have you no feelings at all?' Thus the
conscious life of a woman always has a certain energy of its
own, a kind of imaginative edge. She is by no means content
for things to remain as they are—she takes no pleasure in
this objectivity.

Men and women love differently

The difference extends right into the way we feel. Now we
are starting to look at the transition into soul-life. Rudolf
Steiner once said men and women even love differently. A
woman's love combines wish and an idealized image. A
woman never really loves a man just as he is but as she
would like him to be, or as what she would wish to change
him into; this can go so far that if the man happens to be an
alcoholic the woman actually believes that she will be able
to break him of the habit. Alternatively, she might have

religious needs which he does not share but then thinks: 'Well, that'll come in time.' This is one of the great illusions that woman have about men's religion—that things will come in time! [*Laughter.*] A man's love on the other hand contains wish combined with desire.

Looking at the whole we see once more that the man lives in the tension in what is above and below. He is, as it were, completely male between his lower parts and completely female in his upper parts. In the case of a woman there is more of wholeness since the male aspect in the limbs is compensated by the female aspect and the female aspect in the upper human being is balanced by a male quality. The fundamental constitutions of men and women are completely opposite. There too we have unity and polarity, the straight and the curved. We can deepen this line of thought a little further. But the question does arise: why is the world organized in this way—why are we so different?

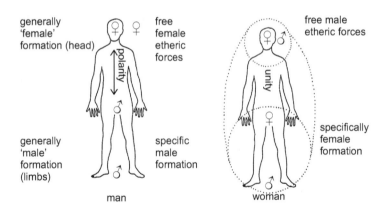

Why are we so different?

We could now go on for many hours about how the differing male and female tendencies are expressed in detail; but a great deal of this is set out in the book *Typisch männlich?*

Typisch weiblich? ['Typically female, typically male'] by Ekkehard Kloehn. It contains examples, such as the fact that women find it easier to recollect two-dimensional images whereas men find it a great deal easier to create three-dimensional images and to remember them. There are also a great deal many more men who find it easier to orientate themselves in space and in the countryside and to use maps, in other words to translate a two-dimensional image into a three-dimensional one in their imagination. Women generally find this a good deal more difficult. My own personal opinion is that this is connected to the fact that the male brain and the whole male body is simply more earthly, more material, heavier, more dense and therefore better adapted to the three-dimensional world; whilst that of the woman is more vital and better adapted to the world of the imagination and pictorial images.

From the division of the sexes to individuality

But why the division into the sexes at all? One could reply in the first place, to enable reproduction to take place. But reproduction takes place in other parts of the living world without the division of organisms into male and female. Asexual reproduction is no longer an option among human beings. It is with all plants and some animals. Any plant, by no means only those which produce fruit and seed, can be propagated from leaves, roots and stems which then produce new shoots. Some of the lower forms of animal life can also do this, in the case of polyps or corals and so on: they simply continue to grow and their cells divide. Unicellular animals can do the same, they simply split and divide and reproduce in that way. They are potentially immortal. It would be a worthwhile biological study to observe how the division of the sexes in the animal kingdom also signals the appearance of mortality in the sense that not every cell is now capable of reproducing itself and of building up a whole organism, but some cells simply have to die. In the human being the last remnant of that immortality is in the germ cells which are potentially immortal in the sense that they can continue to live in a new organism. In primitive organisms every cell has this capacity.

What Rudolf Steiner described as the consequence of the division of the sexes, namely death, can readily be observed in biological phenomena: when living organisms have reached a state of development in which they have lost the capacity for asexual reproduction, the capacity to replicate themselves identically, then their unique quality vanishes at death. They become mortal as individuals. Along with this goes a reduced capacity to regenerate. A sponge can be pressed through a sieve, completely squashed and pulped and will then grow together again on the other side. In the case of lizards which are already highly developed verte-brates only a portion of the tail can regenerate and then only if it is broken in a particular place. In a sense that is where they still have a bud. We human beings can just about heal wounds with a scar, but if any part of us is cut off then there is no budding point out of which a replacement part can grow. All this is due to the fact that the life forces which no longer serve regeneration and reproduction are used to build up the nervous system.

One can observe this in the hierarchy of animals: where primitive animals have a nervous system in the marrow of their spine, their reproductive organs are somewhere in the middle of their body. The more developed the animal is, the more the nervous system is concentrated towards the head and the reproductive organs move down towards the limbs until the polarity can be observed. There is a direct rela-tionship between the development of the nervous system on the one hand and the loss of regenerative ability and the shifting of the reproductive organs towards the opposite pole of the organisms on the other. Thus the division of the sexes is connected with mortality in the organism and is connected with evolution towards a central nervous system in the human being and thus with consciousness. This is after all what has made it possible for us to have ego consciousness.

The ego consciousness of the human being was bought for the price of the division of the sexes. The capacity to think is due to the fact that only half our reproductive forces are used for that purpose. Thus part of it can be used for a conscious soul-life, conception and thinking, and the other parts must be complemented by another individual. Error, sickness and death follow the division of the sexes, but also the possibility of individualization, the possibility of developing an ego consciousness. This is already heralded in the animal hierarchy. All animals which reproduce by germination and not by sexual reproduction are virtually identical. By contrast sexual reproduction facilitates the differentiation of organisms, individual diversity, and finally in the case of the human being, even diversity arising from the activity of the individual – which is yet another development. Rudolf Steiner sets this out very clearly in his book *Theosophy*. The division of the sexes enables us to be individuals. Rudolf Steiner was even more specific and added that the male contribution to reproduction supports the individualizing process and the female contribution supports what is common to the species.[13] Thus individualization like the capacity to think and the capacity to experience ego consciousness, is a fruit and a consequence of the division of the sexes, though sickness and death also follow from it.

The gulf between men and women

Here we have then a fundamental aspect of human existence which is a two-edged sword: on the one hand we owe not only the freedom of the individual to the division of the sexes but also the first and most primitive form of what we call love. Love arises as the tension and attraction between the sexes as a result of their division. The highest values of human existence — love, freedom, individuality, thinking — all arise from the division of the sexes. It is indeed a precondition for our highest values but at the same time, the cause of our greatest problems.

Sexuality is a problem in itself. Sickness and death, one-sidedness, the experience of the gulf, are the results of the difference between man and woman. The gulf between the two is greater than the differences between peoples and races. The man is simply not able to experience what it feels like to live in a woman's body and a woman can also not experience what it feels like to live in a male body. It is beyond the reach of empathy. Even falling in love only gives us the temporary illusion that we can understand each other. The isolation and thus the loneliness of the human being are also consequences of the division of the sexes, even the isolation of the human being from the spiritual world. This is represented very clearly in the old myths which describe the division of the sexes and the consequent Fall, followed by the expulsion from Paradise, showing that as a consequence of the division of the sexes the human being even loses the possibility of being at one with the divine world. That is to say, the most problematic, but also the greatest and most noble aspects of the human condition follow from the division of the sexes.

This division of the sexes preceded all subsequent division among humankind. The division into races after the great flood, the division of the peoples following the Tower of Babel, both these things happen after the division of the sexes. Indeed the division of the sexes even happens before the Fall and in fact makes it possible. The problem is that today every human being assumes in the depths of his soul: 'What I think, what I feel, is the same as what he or she feels'. And then comes the dreadful moment when one has to realize that in fact everything is quite different in the case of the opposite sex. If one does not take account of the fundamentally different organization of the male and female organism it becomes a source of constant misunderstandings and that is before we even begin to consider the distinctions that arise from individuality. In our physical bodies we are immutably man or woman—if we disregard some naturally transsexual cases and some artificial changes of sex which are possible today by means of operations and hormone treatment. The same immutability applies to our vital forces. The soul is also affected by this difference because our soul is incarnated in our body.

Only in respect of the ego of the individual personality are we really equal, potentially equal, not the same but of equal value. However this part of the human being is still rather rudimentary. Rudolf Steiner always refers to this 'baby in the human being', the youngest member of our total being, the weakest and least developed. Indeed if one takes a good look it's even difficult to say where it is. It is very difficult to describe an experience of the ego. And yet this is the only aspect in which we are equal. 95 per cent of our being is not ego and in this 95 per cent we are divided along sexual lines. Naturally the question must arise: if indeed we are so different, right down into the organization of our reproductive system, why should we strive towards lifelong partnership with a person of the opposite sex?

'The fundamental misunderstanding at the beginning of one's first sexual encounter'

To conclude let me present you with two findings from sexual research which make this even clearer. Women aged between 18 and 45 were asked about the motives for their first sexual contact with a man. There were four possible

answers given in multiple choice format. The four possibilities were: curiosity, fear of losing the partner; desire (i.e.
their own libido); reluctance to appear old-fashioned. Then
a similar age-group of men were asked what they thought
the motives of the women might have been. The men's
replies came in as follows: 73 per cent thought it was the
women's own desire; 5 per cent fear of losing the partner;
about 10 per cent curiosity and the remainder reluctance to
appear old-fashioned. That was the reply that men gave to
the question about what, in their opinion, the motives of the
women were for their first sexual contact. In fact 76 per cent
of the women gave the reason as fear of losing their partner
and 6 per cent their own desire. The other two categories we
can disregard because they were the same in both groups,
10 and 5 per cent. What this illustrates is the fundamental
misunderstanding present at the beginning of an intense
relationship!

Now one could ask: What are women up to? Are they
giving the men the wrong impression? Why don't they say
how they feel? [*Members of the audience express a variety of
views.*] But if the main reason is fear of losing the partner
why don't they say so?

Female member of the audience: *It's fear again!*

Exactly. It's fear! Then she will lose him. Precisely — the
primary motive in the woman's soul — this is now well
known in psychology — has to do with relationships, with
'what goes on between them'. Human relationships are as it
were the number one area of interest for the soul of the
woman.

This is not the case with men. Men are married to their
job, to objectivity. The latter is much more important for
them, however curious it might appear, whether in the form
of football, cars or politics. For these things are all external
for them and often the very things to which they have no
relationship. Just think of all the political talk men can
indulge in on matters over which they can have no control!

Just look at how they can get involved in a football match, even though they are not playing and how they suddenly show they do have souls after all!

Can a woman experience desire?

There is often a big question at the beginning of a relationship which men often use more or less as a way of exerting pressure: 'If you don't want to, you don't really love me', as if sexuality were the same as love. We shall come back to this. If men and women have so little in common in their very natures one could ask if a women experiences desire at all, and what is a woman's desire like?

If we follow the distinctions which Rudolf Steiner draws in his *Study of Man*[14] then we can see that there is a will element at work in the body. This he calls instinct, which appears in animals as an organically based form of will which is lived out more or less automatically. At the level of life forces, this will is expressed as drive, and in the soul forces in the astral body, as desire. Human beings do not have an instinct for living together as man and woman. There is no binding form of partnership of the sexes as there is in the case of some animals, but there is a drive.

What exactly is this drive? Purely as a life process it means that something is blossoming, blooming, putting forth leaves. In the case of plants for example, something is growing within and shooting outwards. In a man there are 120 million seeds daily shooting outwards to put forth seeds as it were, quite independently of what is going on in his feeling life. What is the corresponding phenomenon in a woman? Is there something similar striving to put forth shoots in a biological, etheric sense? So does the woman not have a drive? Or is that too hasty a conclusion to draw? [*The audience is silent.*] It is quite clear that in a man this drive is connected with bodily processes: there really is something there striving to put forth shoots. This monthly descent of an ovum, on the other hand, is this a kind of drive like the man has? [*Laughter.*] Men would not be embarrassed to describe how they experience that they have a drive, but how about women?

Female member of the audience: Perhaps it's more of a desire to build a relationship.

That would mean it's much more of a feeling experience, which sometimes strongly takes on the nature of a drive. Does it not also have something of a sucking quality?

Female member of the audience: Yes, the desire to take something in.

That is a soul experience once more! After all, the need of the ovum to take something in is not something a woman actually notices. That would be the biological equivalent in her case. But the ovum is completely passive. It simply doesn't make its presence felt.

A longish pause and then one female member of the audience says: 'Well I can still remember quite clearly that the most important thing for me was to have children and to raise them. That was even more important to me than my career which seemed insignificant by comparison. First raise some children!

So is the woman's drive a drive to have children? Could you agree to that? [*Female member of the audience agrees that it is from her point of view.*] This could be something characteristic. Christa Mewes at any rate maintains that bearing children is the true satisfaction of female desire. With uncomplicated births women frequently describe how the process can often be accompanied by a strong experience of pleasure. She goes on to say that the so-called female orgasm is a fairly artificial business and that even the formation of the organs indicates that it is more of a male process than a female one. Something that has, as it were, been copied and was not originally female. Be that as it may, the mere fact that the sexual drive of the woman and its satisfaction may not be so easily, directly and clearly described, indicates the difference between men and women in this area.

Either – or; both – and

I should like to add another instance of the psychological difference between men and women. You have probably already noticed it yourselves. How does a man think and how does a woman think? A man tends always to think in the categories of 'either – or' and considers that to be logical! [*Laughter.*] And if a woman thinks differently he tends to say: 'You just never think logically. You simply can't think logically'. This pattern of thinking in terms of 'either – or' has produced a whole technologically-based civilization and, most recently, the computer. This functions entirely on the basis of 'either – or'. It is based on a binary principle: current off = no, current on = yes. That's the fundamental principle of the computer. It would be interesting to consider why so few girls sign up for computing courses. I believe quite an important reason is that they instinctively reject the kind of thinking that lies within the machine, because it is not their own. What then is a woman's way of thinking? If a man thinks 'either – or', what does a woman think?

Female member of the audience: '*Both – and*'.

'Both – and', precisely! In other words, the man always thinks exclusively and the woman inclusively. This is a kind of rule of thumb which one could use to observe how differently men and women think in every day life.

One can also observe the difference in how men and women come to decisions. How are decisions made? How often one hears men say 'She can never make up her mind'. Why not? Why do woman generally take longer making decisions? Let us imagine a woman who goes shopping to buy a pair of shoes. She may have an idea of what she would like but is not yet quite certain exactly what. She wants to make up her mind on the basis of what she finds in the shops: she looks at many pairs and goes from one shop to the other. Eventually she goes to the fourth shop and then back to the first, and then she might buy the first or the second pair that she looked at, then three days later brings them back to swap for another pair. [*Laughter.*] That is by no means a caricature. Just look at all the exchanging that goes on after Christmas! Who is it that actually goes and does this? Men would certainly have time if they wanted to but for most of them it is too much bother. Men tend to say: 'I need a pair of shoes, they shouldn't cost more than so and so much, they have to be useful for this or that and they have to be practical — that's it.' One, two or three different criteria form the basis of the eventual decision and it really doesn't matter too much if they end up being a bit on the brown side or a bit on the red side, or if the heels are a bit higher or a bit lower.

Men tend to decide more on the basis of criteria, of conceptual criteria, which are far fewer in number than the manifold phenomena in the world of the senses. Women tend to find the multiplicity of all that can be experienced by the senses much more important than men. This can lead to reproaches being made such as: 'You haven't noticed that I am wearing a new dress!' My wife had a haircut some time ago. Who was it who rushed up to her and said: 'Oh, you have had your hair cut'? Plenty of women, but no men. Why is it so interesting that only women respond to it? There must be a reason for it. Without making any value judgement, it is clear that a woman's soul life is much more directed towards perception and a man's much more directed towards concepts. One could point to many such examples of how our soul life is different and this does not, of course, mean that men have no pleasure in the diversity of the sense world. Nor does it mean that a woman cannot seek the unity of concepts. But this is not the primary orientation of their soul in each case.

Love and sexuality do not have anything to do with each other

Another complicating factor in the question of married life is the business of love. People often say that they know what it is and that they have it. What people experience is falling in love which happens to one like a natural event, and which for a certain time gives one a sensation of being at one with each other – by no means in accordance with reality – which covers and bridges the gulf that normally exists between men and woman. And what a blissful feeling it is, this feeling of being at one with each other! And what could be more natural than to express this feeling of being at one with each other, to intensify and confirm it, than physical closeness?

There is a problem here which is by no means easy to grapple with but since two such distinguished minds as Rudolf Steiner and Erich Fromm have said so, I will also assert that love and sexuality have nothing whatever to do with each other. This might sound odd at first but it is worth penetrating to the truth of the matter, for otherwise the greatest misunderstandings can arise in this area.

One can describe love as a feeling or a condition in which one soul always makes an encouraging, warm, opening gesture towards the other. Just as warmth also makes physical objects expand, the soul warmth of being in love and of love itself makes the human being expand and stretch, initially by way of interests in things and objects but then particularly towards living beings and other humans.

This love contains an additional element as we have already seen: among women there is a natural inclination to wish that the man might yet turn out to be something other than he actually is. So there is a kind of pedagogical eros among women towards men, whom they always wish to educate a little. It is as if men were rough diamonds requiring a last polish from women. We know, however, from *The Philosophy of Spiritual Activity* that it is only we ourselves who can administer this final polish. Nevertheless, it is the case that women are more inclined to try this than men towards women. Men would prefer to have women remain as they are. How often do we hear the reproach; 'You were quite different when I married you. What suddenly got this idea into your head? Why don't we leave everything as it was!' Thus we can see on the one side this pedagogical eros in the love of the woman towards the man that wishes to make him more like her ideal image of a man; an element of wish and fantasy in the love of a woman for a man. On the other side we find an element of desire and possessiveness in the love of a man for a woman. Yet in the physical encounter which necessarily follows from this feeling in the soul it is easy for a certain alienation to arise. Why is this?

Because if you look at the simplest form of physical communication between people then we can say the most basic is sense perception through eye and ear. What do men look at when they look at a woman? What do women look at when they are looking at a man? Do you know that? [*Several listeners call out.*] Women look at men's eyes. Where else? What else is particularly important for a woman? [*More people call out from the audience.*] The hands the face, the mouth. What do men look at? [*Laughter.*] Fine, we'll say no more about that then. If you know already we don't need to elaborate. So each sex has a different point of view. What becomes clear is that the man tends to look more at what is generic in the woman and the woman looks more at the physical expression of what characterizes the soul within, at the physiognomy. So we differ already in the way we look at each other. What accompanies this gaze if we are dealing with lovers is a certain form of possessiveness; in the man's case more grasping, in the woman's case more drawing or sucking. Indeed just consider this peculiar polarity in a woman's being where on the one hand everything is done to ensure she is looked at and then on the other hand, when she is, she doesn't actually like it.

The looks that we exchange already bear within them a grasping tendency. This is desire! And desire actually means that into this opening gesture of sympathy is mixed a portion of antipathy. Antipathy is a closing-off gesture, an exclusive gesture in the soul, one that makes a boundary. Rudolf Steiner once said in his *Theosophy* that the 'fires of desire' constitute that area of the soul in which antipathy still predominates over sympathy. Desire wants a space all of its own, and this desire can already find its way into the manner in which we look at each other. There is a look that seizes hold of its object: more grasping than sucking, more male than female. But the sucking gesture is no less inclined to take hold of its object – let it not be thought after all that women have no desire, it is simply somewhat different in character. All this means is that in the very area in which we communicate as one human to the other, in which we meet each other as beings of soul and spirit, via the intermediary of physical sense perception, there is at once an element that seeks to interrupt an objective perception, a true meeting of beings.

Now one can make a certain effort to become aware of this in oneself and perhaps even exercise a certain degree of control: how do I look at and listen to another human being? In the case of listening it is actually a little easier. We are not by nature so inclined to experience desire in our listening as we are in looking. 'Whoever looks at a woman with desire commits adultery with her in his heart.' Why should this be? We shall come back to this when we have spoken about marriage.

If we now go a step further and look at what happens when lovers take each other by the hand, then we see that that too can be the gesture that makes a bridge from one soul to another; where, as they say, something comes across. But it can also be that actually nothing comes across but that this is the first step towards taking hold of the other and holding them captive.

A teacher should use the daily handshake with his pupils as an organ of perception of the spiritual, soul and physical well-being of the child. But that is a path of development. If things go a little further and the lovers embrace then they are taking further what started with clasped hands: they are experiencing each other through the sense of touch.

The sense of touch

The sense of touch is characterized by the fact that we actually don't take into ourselves anything of what it is we have touched. With hearing, even with seeing, but particularly with smelling and tasting it is otherwise. Something of the essence of what is perceived penetrates into us. With the sense of hearing, the being of what is perceived sounds forth and gives a message that we receive. With smelling and tasting we actually take into ourselves something of the substance of what is perceived. And with the sense of touch it is not actually the things themselves that we perceive but rather the change that these things bring about in our own bodies. The sense of touch is characterized by the fact that it actually gives an experience of ourselves. Now if this goes to and fro in the form of affection between a man and a woman it can also be a bridge that makes possible a soul-to-soul encounter. But the sense of touch is organized in such a way that it is very easy for us to start experiencing only what goes on in our own body. The sense of touch therefore is an area in which the human being is actually thrown back on himself.

When the relationship then becomes a sexual one, it inevitably ends up as more or less absolute perception of oneself in isolation and it is in the nature of the thing that nothing more comes across, but that each person experiences only what is going on in their own body. That is to say, when the partners engage in sex the very opposite takes place of what is the fundamental soul gesture of love. The awful thing is that the same word is used for both things today and it is all called love. Strictly in terms of sex it really doesn't matter at all who the other individual is. In a recent course on marriage for young people a young man once said: 'To be honest, when it comes to the crunch, it really doesn't matter who the other person is.' That is of course a typically male thought, since women have a greater tendency to experience things as a whole, which doesn't necessarily apply to men in the same way. For a man the personal element is more likely to go missing in this area. Nevertheless I think we can see that in what passes from one person to another by means of the body, the fundamental gesture of love is affected by something that actually destroys love itself.

This was not always so. The process of sexual union was once described in these terms: 'And he knew his wife'. Clearly there have been times in the evolution of humanity when this process led to human beings encountering each other in a higher, spiritual sense. Rudolf Steiner has also described it in these terms but said that this only really applied before the Great Flood. Clearly we have lost a level of encounter that was once possible in the sexual act.

Thus we can conclude: in the process that is commonly thought of as being the greatest expression of love, there lies an element which turns this love into its opposite. One can see this peculiar ambivalence, this peculiar paradox that lies within the act itself. However, not many people are inclined to point this out nowadays. Erich Fromm and Rudolf Steiner are only two people who talk of love and sexuality as two completely separate things. If it should be so however, then the seeds of destruction of a human relationship lie in the very process that follows naturally from the attraction of the sexes.

Why then contemplate lifelong monogamy?

2. The Sacrament of Marriage in The Christian Community

Earlier we looked at the 'moral intuition' of marriage as one might imagine it. Now we are going to take this a step further in respect of the sacrament of marriage.

The threefold resolve to wed

One can say that there are three levels on which one takes the resolve to wed: the first is the resolve of two human beings to live together, which in most cases comes about quite unconsciously, that is to say, on the basis of feelings and needs.

It is already on a different level when two people decide to go to the Registry Office. Anyone who is familiar with the ways of the world will know that this step has considerable consequences, by no means easy for men to accept when it comes to divorce; these are connected above all with the material aspects of the arrangement: maintenance, alimony, shared pensions etc. But when one goes to the Registry Office, all the aspects of this agreement are underwritten in advance; the terms and conditions of separation are agreed in advance. That is about all that civil marriage entails.

While I was a student, a friend of mine who was studying law had just begun learning about marital and family rights. At the time I had no idea about the law in relation to marriage and I asked him what on earth the law had to do with it. His answer was: 'If the marriage goes well, you don't need the law; and if it doesn't go so well, the law won't help much either'. That was his somewhat droll interpretation. The law is nowadays really only involved when it comes to divorce, when the marriage has failed. In former times it was different. In those days the law positively determined the contents of the marriage: both the partners in the marriage had an obligation to love and be faithful to each other, to raise children etc. etc. I don't know what other injunctions there were, nor indeed what there might still be in other countries and constitutions, but in the Federal Republic of Germany, the law relating to marriage is one of the most liberal one could imagine. Nowadays no reference is made to the content of the marriage; there is only a formal recognition of the fact that the couple are living together and running a joint household.

Question: *How long has this law been in existence?*

Since the reform of the marriage law in 1977. But the principle was established well before that in the sense that people said that the state and the law had no business trying to determine the questions, aims and ideals of individual people, i.e. to intervene in matters of people's outlook on life. This is actually no bad thing, for it is a small step in the direction of the threefolding of the social order. After all it cannot be up to the law to determine what the content of a marriage should be. This is something that people have to work out through their own intuition and their own capacities. The trouble is that they are not yet used to this, and one of the reasons it is so difficult is that the institution of marriage has been regulated for hundreds of years.

At all events, this second resolve to marry is the one that links up with my acknowledgement of the legal consequences of the step. The first resolve is really an external one, relating to the economic life. It is a step towards an economic community, involving for example the sharing of the housekeeping, and it relates to the human being as a being who has economic needs. If you read Christof Lindenau's book *Soziale Dreigliederung: Der Weg zu einer lernenden Gesellschaft* ['The threefold social order, the way to a learning society'] then you will see that the human being can be looked at from three points of view:

—as a being with needs,
—as a being with a right to self-determination,
—as a being with capacities.

If two people simply move in together, then it is because they have a need to do so. One could also say: such a partnership involves the primarily economic function of meeting each other's needs. Most people who live in this way would, of course, hotly reject this way of characterizing their situation. But if one takes a look at this arrangement it is usually rather like that.

If, on the other hand, one appears before a legally constituted body and signs a contract between two partners who have equal rights and are both of age—this is something which our present law relating to marriage permits—then one is founding a little legal community.

Now one could take a third step and join together as spiritually endowed, moral, self-conscious beings. One could take the resolve to unite spiritually in the sacrament of marriage. One does not need to. It is—one would hope—an even freer resolve than the one taken at the Registry Office. And if it is not so then the priests of the Christian Community have the task to make it as free as possible in that they urge the people concerned not to marry at once. Why should that be? So that what we discussed yesterday, the moral intuition of marriage, the idea of marriage has time to develop, which is then referred to directly in the sacrament of marriage in the Christian Community.

Turning the work of earth into work of the spirit

To begin with there is a table with a red cloth and on it a picture of the resurrected Christ. In front of the picture lie two sticks with a red ribbon. The bride and groom and the two witnesses are seated before the table. The first words spoken by the priest contain within them the signature of all that is to follow. In these words the being of the Christ is characterized in a way that is appropriate and necessary for the sacrament of marriage. Through his deed of sacrifice the Christ transforms the work of earth into work of the spirit, which is in fact the real task of marriage: transforming what is earthly into something spiritual, raising up what is merely earthly into the spirit. The sacrament consists of bringing about this transformation through one's own deed of sacrifice! Initially it is a deed of the Christ. A marriage, however, means nothing less than that the parties to it have the will to continue this deed individually to the best of their ability, and in relation to the Being whose deed this was, who continues to perform this deed and who hopes that human beings will link their forces to this deed of transforming work of earth into the work of the spirit!

The resolve

As the ritual proceeds there follow two more passages which introduce the question to the bride and groom and which bear the signature of what has already been said. The question has its own peculiar character: it is no longer a matter of 'Are you willing to marry so-and-so etc.' but rather a question of whether one is prepared to make community of life with the other partner one of the resolves with which one walks in the world of spirit.

So now it is a question of resolve. In the context of the various aspects of the human will that Rudolf Steiner describes and whose three lowest forms we referred to yesterday — instinct, drive and desire — a resolve is the very highest, the very best that it is possible for the human being to express through the spiritual members of his being,

because it has to do with the new body, with the spiritualized body which Rudolf Steiner describes as Spirit
Man. The highest manifestation of the human will is
addressed here and is called upon. The character of these
resolves is made clear in the reference to the fact that they
are resolves with which one walks in the world of the spirit.
There are those in the Christian Community who take the
view — after all we can exercise freedom in respect of
doctrine — that the way this is put in the marriage ritual
suggests that the resolve referred to is one taken before
birth. Any walking in the world of the spirit we may have
done will have been before birth. But if one focuses on what
is said more exactly, one notices that the verb walk is not in
the past tense but in the present. So in this case it is a present
walking in the world of the spirit and not a past one.

Do we actually walk in the world of the spirit? Well, one
could reply: 'Yes, we walk in the world of the spirit every
night'; but then they would be nightly resolves in the world
of the spirit. Perhaps it is more appropriate to think of this
resolve of the will more in terms of the kind of walking in
the world of the spirit which is possible for today's
consciousness. This is what we spoke of yesterday: that one
can raise oneself up to an idea. This idea does not have to be
compelling, but one which is freely taken hold of in love
and — if one so desires — may become a resolve.

In the sacrament of marriage each of the two partners is
asked if they are willing to make community of life with the
other partner such a resolve. A challenge such as this might
well lead one to ask: 'Do I actually have such resolves which
are held so consciously as aims, as ideas, that I can say of
them that I walk with them in the world of the spirit?' This
would after all mean that they have a separate existence in
the spiritual world and continue even when I have fallen
asleep or died! Or are they merely resolves which are
significant only in respect of earthly life? — A very particular
kind of resolve is referred to when we speak of the resolves

with which we walk in the world of the spirit. It becomes all the more precise when the individual is addressed as 'you' directly, not in terms of 'one' as a general capacity to walk in the world of the spirit, but rather: 'Do you yourself wish this, is it *your* resolve, is it *your* idea? Do *you* wish to walk with this in the world of the spirit?'

Raising the idea of marriage to an ideal

It follows then that the key question whether the idea of marriage, which leads to the resolve to marry, is merely something one has read up, something one has taken on board, or is merely some kind of dressing; or whether it is something one really owns and wills oneself. To make such an idea into an ideal involves making so strong a connection with the idea that it becomes the content of one's ego, of one's own person. As Rudolf Steiner points out in his *Theosophy*, the ego attains to its being and meaning through those things with which it unites itself. If the ego is exclusively concerned with physical things, it will gradually die. On the other hand, if it is connected with spiritual things it will gradually become immortal. But this means that if you make a connection between this idea of community of life and your own ego then it will become a constituent part of your own ego, and thus if you drop this idea you are actually dropping a part of your own ego. Do you then indeed make this threefold idea of community of life with the other partner—whose name is mentioned during the course of the ritual—into the content of your resolve, into the content of your own ego, which you would gradually lose if you dropped this idea again? We can see at once that it is very rare for us to make resolves of which we could say that we walk with them in the world of the spirit. It is an enormous task even to strive towards such ideas, such resolve.

Then follows the 'Yes' of the bride and groom. Naturally anyone can easily say 'Yes', and it is an important task in the preparation of the marriage — perhaps even the main task — to work towards making this yes, a real, a genuine, an effective one. This means one has to try to achieve the clearest possible consciousness of what such a resolve means, of whether it is really present and if one genuinely does will it so. The rituals of the Christian Community are fashioned in such a way that every word spoken in them makes it clear that the important thing is the inner participation of each individual soul, of each individual consciousness. Naturally this applies particularly to the consciousness of those who are directly concerned.

The word 'Yes' is spoken in the second part of the marriage ritual. It is a process of heightening awareness which is now intensified in a third, rather larger part which is directed towards the witnesses.

The admonition of the witnesses

Once the bride and groom, whose names are mentioned seven times in the course of the ritual, have set the seal on their community of life with the word 'Yes', words of admonition are directed towards the witnesses, not to the wedded couple. It is said that the ears have heard and the eyes have seen how — and now there is a slight differentiation — the spirit world of this man and the soul spirit of this woman have united in community of life. There appears an initial slight differentiation in the spiritual quality of this resolve which was not evident earlier on when the resolve was formed and when the word 'Yes' was pronounced. So even when man and woman raise themselves up into the world of the spirit, there is a slight shading towards a will quality in the case of the man and more towards a soul quality in the case of the woman. So it is once more clearly pointed out that two people, the witnesses, have experienced something with their physical eyes and ears here on earth which also has a spiritual character: that a resolve has been perceived which the participants stand by in the spiritual world. The fact that such a resolve has manifested in the earthly world of the senses is of such significance that it is once more urgently impressed upon the witnesses.

And then comes the actual admonition of the witnesses, with the thrice repeated words: 'Never let...': words with an edge to them unlike almost any other words to be found in the sacraments of the Christian Community. Something similar appears in the sacrament of the ordination of priests when the words are spoken 'Only if...' These words contain a kind of exclusivity, a kind of sternness. Never may the awareness leave the souls of these people, who wish to be witnesses, of what they have there seen and heard. When somebody is a witness this is the meaning normally attributed to the phrase: 'He has seen it, he has heard it'. In the sacrament of marriage however, it is not the same as at the Registry Office, where the witnesses document with their signatures that everything is official; they are witnesses to the quality of the resolve in the world of the senses, in the earthly world. Thus the witnesses also have to be just as involved in the preparation as the bride and the groom otherwise they could only bear witness to the fact that two people have said 'Yes' or 'No'. One does not need to be a witness in a religious sense to do this. Rather they must bear witness to the fact that the following quality accompanied the word 'Yes': 'I have experienced this, I know it!' It is the task of the witnesses to sustain in their consciousness the following thought: 'These two people once made this resolve and I was there. I have experienced how this resolve was clothed in earthly words.' That is the one task they have.

The living aid of the witnesses

There follows immediately the second task given to the witnesses with the warning that they must never lose the will to help and provide active aid and that they promise this before God for the life of the bride and groom. This promise within the sacrament is as clear as it could possibly be. The witnesses vow to give active aid. Newly weds need all kinds of help. When they are young, the arrival of every child almost always involves a move. It is nice to have friends who are willing to help. Life is made easier. We could summarize this as an outer, earthly form of help. But this cannot be the content of a religious vow. There is another kind of support which a married couple urgently need. It is the soul support of warm, human friendship. But there too one does not need to promise this within the context of a sacrament. Physical and emotional support are really the duty of fellow human beings, of fellow Christians. And if the witnesses live far away then they cannot help with the move. Another good friend would help with that.

But the active aid which is promised for the life of the wedded couple, what does this actually mean? What do you imagine this to mean? It has to be something new, not just a matter of consciousness but a fact of life — living aid. It consists in prayer for the wedded couple! A colleague of mine once put it very strongly in these words: 'If the witnesses were really to pray regularly for the married couple, then no marriage would break down.' I would not perhaps put it quite so strongly, because it can indeed depend on quite other things. But it is certainly right and good to emphasize that the task of community of life is too great for the two involved. How can intercession help?

If we can imagine the couple and their witnesses, then intercession does not mean that one sends them good wishes, but rather that one directs one's love, one's attention, one's consciousness to the angels of the two concerned and to the angel of the family, of the marriage. And this has the consequence that the beings of the third hierarchy, the angels, both those of the individuals and that of the partnership, are in a position to let something flow into the life of the people concerned which previously would not have been possible. New destiny, free destiny can be brought about in this way. Living active aid – and input as it were from the spiritual world into the life of these two people. To be a witness therefore means that one is actually co-creating the marriage, that one is helping to bring it about, not just that one says one has witnessed the process, one has been there, one has seen, one has heard, one holds it in one's consciousness – but rather: I am making myself co-responsible for the development of community of life between these two people, co-responsible by means of the religious activity to which I here commit myself.

The conclusion of this part of the service speaks once more of the 'life' of the wedded couple – another reference to the sphere of life, of biography – and of their search for community of life before the eyes of their witnesses. Not that they have by any means found it already – that they live together is the first step, the Registry Office the second, the marriage the third. They have not reached the end of the process, but rather the search has now really begun. Only now does the process move into a new realm, a new sphere.

The sphere of imagination

This brings to a conclusion the first three parts of the marriage ritual, each of which essentially addresses the consciousness of those present in sober conceptual terms. There now follow three parts which really belong in another sphere, in which other aspects of the ritual take effect: the sphere of imagination, of pictures. Three images occur: the image of the ring, the image of the crossed sticks and the image of the Risen One. First of all, the rings of the bride and groom are crossed over and placed on the table before the other partner. Each will have previously worn a ring with their own name inscribed on it and now have taken it off.

The ring which rounds the corners of life

Reference is now made to this ring that will round off the corners of life. This is another point worth noting, that precisely within the sacrament of marriage there is mention of the rough edges of life. This means that there is no assumption that everything will go smoothly. It is understood that there will be rough edges and sharp corners in the community of life. What is important is that something lives in it which can unite the individual with the whole. One could take the view that as a married couple one forms part of a kind of whole. But if the image of the ring is taken seriously enough one sees that each partner receives a ring, rather than both of them sharing one ring. For if that were the case one would be bound to one's partner. Each of the two receives a ring and that means that each is called upon to become whole within the marriage. As the rings are put on it is said first to the woman and then to the man that the ring will join their forces and bind their hearts together. These are two separate areas of human life: the joining of forces has to do with life forces and the binding together of the hearts has to do with the realm of the soul. The roundness, the image of unity, has to do with the realm in which the woman is already more at home. Later a different realm is addressed in the shape of the two sticks. There we are faced with two straight objects with the cross, with the corner. But first and foremost these two symbols have to do with the fact that there is a task that lies before the couple of joining their forces, of binding their hearts together, of establishing community in the realm of their soul and life forces. The golden ring of unity in which the name of each is engraved is a symbol of the binding of hearts and joining of soul forces. Each partner receives a ring with the name of the other engraved in it which means that each partner feels answerable in his deeds to the ego, to the being of the other person, to serve that being in such a way that the result is a unity, a higher unity, a golden oneness. One no longer has one's own ring on one's finger, but the ring of the other. This expresses in picture form the intention of the marriage: that each will feel called upon, as we mentioned yesterday in our discussion of the idea, to be active in support of the progress and development and ego of the other.

The sticks that bind together what is separate

Then follows the passage with the two sticks which previously lay side by side. They are bound together with a ribbon in the shape of a cross and held aloft before the couple. This is where the ritual mentions that what was formerly separate is now bound together. What was formerly individual and separate is now united in the image of the two sticks which are tied together. Then we hear that what was bound together in spirit—that is how the resolved is characterized here—may shine into the realm of the soul for community of life. We see here how the resolve passes from above downwards. And the fact that this spiritual union takes hold of the whole of human life is witnessed by a divine spirit. This process must be continued and cultivated, the uniting gesture must continually be sought after and cultivated, which proceeds from spirit union in the realm of the soul into community of life. It is not a single act but one that must be continually renewed and repeated.

This is why marriage must be understood as a life process. It is only a beginning. What the man might find easier to do initially, namely to raise himself up to this ideal, must now be brought into the soul life. In the first lecture we spoke about the difference between men and women. The woman's oneness is found in the forces of life and of the soul and the man's polarity exists between the spirit and the body and this must be joined together again in a balanced and harmonious unity, in which one can see the overcoming of the division of mankind into two sexes. One could even rephrase the words of the New Testament to the effect that 'what God has separated into two sexes, mankind must now bring together again'. This process is so important that a divine being directs its attention to it, that a divine being looks upon what human beings are doing in this realm. Full of expectation the gods are asking 'Will human beings take up the task that follows from the fact that the divine world has divided humanity into male and female? Will there be human beings who take this task upon themselves?'

In the light of the Risen One

The third image refers to the Risen One and with it comes this remarkable and often misunderstood reference to the man going before and the woman following after. The man is told that he should shine before the woman with the light which the Risen One lets shine in his spirit. The woman is asked to follow him in the light which the Risen One lets shine in her soul. This is not a revised version of an old form of chauvinism, nor does it indicate that any superiority or right of decision is being conferred on the man. On the contrary, we are talking about a sacrament, a religious act. If a man wishes to be religious, then he must see a need for it in his mind, otherwise as a modern human being he can make no relationship to the Risen One. If he can't see the point of it in his mind, he cannot build a relationship to the Risen One. This does not need to be total enlightenment but at least a glimmer of the light of the Risen One. Then he is in a position to light the way because this light has a more objective quality, although it is constantly in danger of lifting off from reality and of disappearing in abstraction from the other realms of life.

The woman has the capacity to channel her forces into her life because she lives more strongly in the area where the soul is connected with the body, where the spiritual members are connected with the physical members of the human being, and where the man experiences a separation.

Interruption: Things can dawn on her!

Yes, but the light shines differently in the soul and the spirit. For a woman it is not so necessary that it shines up here so intellectually, so spiritually, conceptually and ideally. It can shine directly into her soul. This is why there are so many more women in religious and spiritual gatherings because it is more easily and more directly possible for the Risen One to shine into the soul of the woman.

Nevertheless it must go beyond this and that is why the woman is asked to follow the man. There is nothing negative about following, nor is lighting the way in itself positive. It is more a matter of what is possible for each partner to contribute in a religious sense to community of life out of the circumstances of their present incarnation. Moreover in each case when the following and the lighting of the way are mentioned, the name is mentioned with them as an indication that it is the higher ego of the other person that is referred to. Not: follow his whims and his moods; but follow him as far as the light of the Risen One shines in his spirit.

Question: Given that we are today in the age of the consciousness soul are not both activities possible for each partner?

This is the task of community of life and to that each must

bring what he can. Rudolf Steiner once said that one should give to the other what one is good at. The spiritual aspect of the man can be very far removed from reality, very clear and distinct, but nevertheless lacking in life. This on the other hand would be the quality that the woman could bring to community of life. Not of course out of a dull and dreamy, natural sense for religion but rather in her following as she links up with the spiritual and ideal. This is the opportunity for further development that is open to each. The man is further ahead in life in this aspect of spirituality, not individually but because he is a man, a male human being. The price he had to pay for this was a deeper Fall. That is why it is much more of a struggle for him to reach it at all. One could say more about the consequences of the Fall for women in modern times, but this is not the place for it.

The blessing

The next part of the ritual draws attention to the particular spiritual Being who is waiting for what can come from the human being through His grace, as is mentioned at the beginning and is then made explicit after a personal address in the last major part of the ritual. The Christ sees the binding, blessing 'Yes' of the bridal couple.

The blessing consists in the fact that each says 'Yes' with this in mind. Each has found him or herself. The quality of the resolve, the quality of the word is a blessing. It is the first blessing that is uttered at all. Only then does a blessing in the more usual sense, a blessing for the future destiny of the two come into the service. The blessing of the Trinity comes when the human beings have blessed each other with the word 'Yes'. Then there comes once more a look back at the earthly meeting of the bridal couple. That took place in the past, but it did after all make it possible for the present resolve to be taken.

Towards the end of the service there is once more a threefold blessing which is bestowed on the soul forces of the bridal couple, for their happiness in life and for the benefit and happiness of the whole of humanity. The blessing has become happiness in life but this does not happen of its own accord. For the light of the spirit to shine, for the souls' inwardness of heart to radiate outwards, it is necessary for human beings to strive upwards towards the Trinity. That is to say, to establish relationship to the world out of which the soul forces can be fructified and spiritualized so that the life forces, the etheric bodies of the human beings can be transformed. The human being must strive towards this ever anew. The marriage is not blessed by virtue of the wedding having taken place, but rather the wedding is the point of departure for this willingness to act out of self-sacrifice, for this transforming of the earthly into the spiritual to be constantly practised and continued in every subsequent Act of Consecration of Man.[15]

The whole thing can only succeed if a religious life is cultivated as part of the partnership or community of life. Otherwise the differences between our life bodies that have been with us since the Creation will bump up against each other and lead to strife and oppression. Progress will only be made if a process of transformation takes place as a result of turning for help towards the divine world. This cannot be a 'once-in-a-lifetime' act. For then it would not work down into the depths of community of life, into the depths of our etheric forces, but would simply remain on the surface of our soul life and spiritual intentions.

This community of life can then succeed if it is striven for together with the wider community, with the congregation, with the sacramental community and when it is supported by the intercession of the witnesses and a regular, shared religious life. It can bring happiness in life to the couple and health and happiness to the whole of humanity. It actually has an impact on the people around it, on its environment!

It is possible to experience how community of life can radiate its good qualities outward, how it can support other destinies. It begins to become a reality that the human being is a co-creator in the second half of evolution, that what the gods have put asunder can be re-united — not without the gods but with their help!

The conclusion of the marriage ritual is the threefold gesture of blessing and the 'So be it. Amen'. There we have the whole of the sacrament before us.

Notes

1. For a fuller description of the human being as an entity of body, soul and spirit, see Rudolf Steiner's *Theosophy* (New York: Anthroposophic Press, 1994).
2. *Erziehung und Unterricht aus Menschenerkenntnis*, GA 302a (Dornach: Rudolf Steiner Verlag, 1993).
3. *Soul Economy and Waldorf Education*, lecture 13 (New York/London: Anthroposophic Press/Rudolf Steiner Press, 1986).
4. Barbara Sichtermann, *Femininity, The Politics of the Personal* (Polity Press, 1986).
5. See Rudolf Steiner, *Pastoral Medicine*, lecture 3 (New York: Anthroposophic Press, 1987).
6. See Rudolf Steiner, *Karmic Relationships*, Vol. VI, lecture 8 (London: Rudolf Steiner Press, 1971).
7. London: Rudolf Steiner Press, 1992. Also published as *Intuitive Thinking as a Spiritual Path* (New York: Anthroposophic Press, 1995).
8. Also published as *An Outline of Esoteric Science* (New York: Anthroposophic Press, 1997).
9. GA 54 (Dornach: Rudolf Steiner Verlag, 1983).
10. New York: Anthroposophic Press, 1982.
11. Ibid.
12. Following the first publication of this interview in German, Gädeke received much correspondence from people challenging his view on child/parent contact in the case of separated parents. This led him to insert a note in following editions explaining that he had subsequently revised his view. To avoid confusion, in this English edition we have worked his note into the main text. The portion of the original interview which has now been edited from the main body of the book, in which he expounds his *previous* view on this question, is as follows:

   W. Gädeke: I am aware that I am taking the opposite view of many psychologists and also of current legislation: I don't think anything at all of the access rights as they are handled today! I have seen it confirmed to me often enough that children who are, in accordance with these access rights, mostly with their mother, then with their father during the holidays, later again with their mother, and so forth, find these changes tremendously difficult. And therefore I think that it would be preferable for the children to be allowed the chance to build up this etheric sheath which they would normally have with both parents, as far as possible exclusively with either the father or mother.

I have been told by a psychologist who deals with such access arrangements that the children—no matter what the marriage was like, however brutal and catastrophic it may have been—will always say: 'I wish Mum and Dad got together again.' There is absolutely no doubt about that, for it is connected with the fact that children need an intact etheric sheath.

If it is no longer intact they should at least in the first seven years, in my view also in the second seven-year-span remain exclusively with one of the parents. I also think that the other parent ought to disappear until after the confirmation. Then children will start asking about their father or their mother, and a very different, far more free relationship to the other parent may be built up. However, as I mentioned already, I know that my point of view is clearly at odds with the feelings of mothers and fathers in such matters and that most people will not heed this advice even though it would be better to do so.

W.W.: One ought to try and come to an objective assessment of what, from the point of view of the child, would be the best for the child and not what parents might wish for.

W. Gädeke: Yes, the difficulties arise because normally only the soul aspect is taken into consideration. Of course it is desirable from that point of view that a child should experience mother and father, and that's why it is said: if the child cannot experience them together, then it should at least be able to experience them separately, which is provided for by the access rights legislation. But the etheric aspect is not taken into account at all in these considerations. And this is the most important, the more far-reaching aspect in the first fourteen years.

It does not mean, after all, that the father—if the child is living with the mother — does not need to care for the child; he can nurture a soul-spiritual relationship with the child even if he does not see the child. He can give the child something, he can pray for his child.

W.W.: But doesn't this mean a one-sided development for the children concerned?

W. Gädeke: Certainly, but what counts here is the question of which is the lesser evil. When the children stay with just one parent, then this is the lesser evil. All the difficulties experienced in connection with today's divorce 'orphans' did not come up in the case of the war widows, for example, who raised their children alone, where the father was totally absent. The problem in such situations is not as acute as it is when he is around and at the same time not around. For then a painful wound remains which is torn open again and again; this can manifest in many different ways, such as bed-wetting right into the second seven-year-span.

W.W.: Does it matter which of the parents is the one?

W. Gädeke: I would say that it definitely does matter in the first seven-year-span, especially if you also consider Rudolf Steiner's indication that in that phase of life the etheric body is not yet born and is still connected with the mother. I would normally advise that the children remain with the mother during that time. But there may be cases, such as mental instability of the mother, where it would be preferable for the child to live with the father.

The father really comes into his own in the third seven-year-span. Very often the children themselves seek out their father then; for at that age they look for and need the stronger will and forming forces of the father.

13. See Rudolf Steiner, *Spiritual Science and Medicine*, lecture 10 (London: Rudolf Steiner Press, 1975).
14. London: Rudolf Steiner Press, 1966. Also published as *The Foundations of Human Experience* (New York: Anthroposophic Press, 1996).
15. The common service of The Christian Community church.